How to Communicate With Your Spouse

The 7-Step Guide to Having a Successful and Happy Relationship: Discover the Secrets to Rekindling Your Love Again

Michael B Daniels

© Copyright 2022 - All rights reserved.

The content contained within this book may not be reproduced, duplicated or transmitted without direct written permission from the author or the publisher.

Under no circumstances will any blame or legal responsibility be held against the publisher, or author, for any damages, reparation, or monetary loss due to the information contained within this book, either directly or indirectly.

Legal Notice:

This book is copyright protected. It is only for personal use. You cannot amend, distribute, sell, use, quote or paraphrase any part, or the content within this book, without the consent of the author or publisher.

Disclaimer Notice:

Please note the information contained within this document is for educational and entertainment purposes only. All effort has been executed to present accurate, up to date, reliable, complete information. No warranties of any kind are declared or implied. Readers acknowledge that the author is not engaged in the rendering of legal, financial, medical or professional advice. The content within this book has been derived from various sources. Please consult a licensed professional before attempting any techniques outlined in this book.

By reading this document, the reader agrees that under no circumstances is the author responsible for any losses, direct or indirect, that are incurred as a result of the use of the information contained within this document, including, but not limited to, errors, omissions, or inaccuracies.

Table of Contents

INTRODUCTION 1
    THE HONEYMOON PHASE 2
    HITTING THE BUMPY ROAD 3
    IT ALL FALLS APART 4
    THE ULTIMATE GUIDE FOR A SUCCESSFUL RELATIONSHIP 6

CHAPTER 1: STEP 1—WHY ARE WE THIS WAY? 9
    HOW DOES THE MALE BRAIN DIFFER FROM THE FEMALE BRAIN? 10
    UPBRINGING AND PAST TRAUMA 13
    REWIRING THE BRAIN FOR BETTER UNDERSTANDING AND EFFECTIVE COMMUNICATION 18
    KEY TAKEAWAYS 21
    APPLICATION WORKBOOK 1 22

CHAPTER 2: STEP 2—THE COMMUNICATION GAP 25
    HOW BIG IS THE PROBLEM? 26
    HOW DO I CONNECT WITH MY PARTNER? 30
    WHAT LEADS TO A COMMUNICATION BREAKDOWN? 32
    WHAT ARE THE COMMON TRIGGERS THAT LEAD TO RELATIONSHIP DISAGREEMENTS? 40
    KEY TAKEAWAYS 43
    APPLICATION WORKBOOK—2 44

CHAPTER 3: STEP 3—THE MAGIC INGREDIENTS 47
    HOW CAN PAYING ATTENTION DRASTICALLY IMPROVE MY RELATIONSHIP? 48
    HOW DO I GET THEM TO LISTEN TO ME? 52
    VALIDATING YOUR PARTNER'S FEELINGS 54
    THE SECRET INGREDIENT TO A HAPPY RELATIONSHIP 56
    KEY TAKEAWAYS 58
    APPLICATION WORKBOOK—3 59

CHAPTER 4: STEP 4–STUCK IN THE MUD 63
    EMOTIONAL STATE: HOW DOES THIS AFFECT MY RELATIONSHIP? 64
        How Do I Overcome My Emotional State? 65
    DIFFERENT WAYS YOU CAN CALM YOURSELF IN AN EMOTIONAL STATE 67
        Take a Deep Breath 68
        Maintain a Thought Journal 68
        Go for a Warm Bath 69
        Meditate for a Minute 69

THE POWER OF A PAUSE BUTTON 70
   The Pause Agreement: Hold It Right There, We Need to Pause! 72
KEY TAKEAWAYS 73
APPLICATION WORKBOOK—4 74

CHAPTER 5: STEP 5–REMOVE ALL OBSTACLES 77

IMPORTANCE OF FORGIVENESS IN A RELATIONSHIP 78
HOW DOES FORGIVENESS HELP WITH SOFTENING THE HEART? 81
THE WAY WE TALK TO EACH OTHER 83
KEY TAKEAWAYS 85
APPLICATION WORKBOOK—5 86

CHAPTER 6: STEP 6–DEVELOP AN IRON TRUST 89

HOW DO I DEVELOP A SAFE ENVIRONMENT FOR MY PARTNER? 90
   Three Ways You Can Rebuild Trust In Your Relationship 91
   Developing a Safe Environment for Your Partner 92
CHECKING IN WITH YOUR PARTNER TO BUILD TRUST 94
   Why Is Check-In Important? 95
KEY TAKEAWAYS 96
APPLICATION WORKBOOK—6 96

CHAPTER 7: STEP 7–REINVENTING YOURSELVES 99

PULLING IT ALL TOGETHER 99
THE ART OF REKINDLING THE FIRE: HOW DO WE BUILD OUR FUTURE TOGETHER? 100
KEY TAKEAWAYS 102

CONCLUSION 103

REFERENCES 105

Introduction

Love. That one word makes us feel happy and whole at the same time. It all starts with the little things, the nicknames we call each other, the flirting, and falling in love. It is amazing how love makes us feel like we can do anything in life and go anywhere. This is, until it all starts to fall apart at some point. Most of the relationships today start with falling in love, but many fall out of love due to a big communication gap, misunderstanding, and constant fighting. In this book, we will address all of these sensitive areas that affect our relationships and how we can strengthen our connection with our significant others.

We will start this book by introducing our couple Noah and Emma, who will serve as the best example throughout this entire book. We will be breaking down this subject by addressing the various issues that every single couple faces in the early and later stages of their relationship and how they can overcome this by simply using certain techniques. There will be an assessment in the form of the workbooks at the end of each chapter to help you evaluate your situation and work on yourself to keep your relationship healthy and happy with your significant other. Before jumping into the next chapter, let us break down the two phases of relationships using our favorite couple. After understanding our couple's dilemma, there will be a brief overview of how each chapter will progress to help you strengthen your relationship. Before you reach the end of this book, you will learn how to evaluate your feelings and move your relationship with your spouse forward the right way.

The Honeymoon Phase

Falling in love with your significant other is just like living the Hollywood dream; those flying sparks, late-night dinners, and romantic kisses. It is just like being on cloud nine where nothing can bring you down. The honeymoon phase almost seems like a fairytale where you are living with the person of your dreams till reality comes crashing down. This is exactly what happened to our happy couple Noah and Emma, who were madly in love a year ago, right before their relationship started to fall apart.

Right before we jump into the whole mess, let us rewind to see what happened exactly. Noah and Emma were yet another couple who met on a blind date which was supposed to be terrible. Noah was an introvert, which meant he would avoid putting himself in a sticky situation. His friend forced him to go on this date, which could only have one outcome: disaster. Noah rarely dated throughout his college years, so suddenly being set up on a blind date gave him the jitters. But all these jitters went straight out of the window when he saw a beautiful brunette walk through the cafe door.

Emma was a confident person who would never shy away from voicing her thoughts and always put everything on the line to help other people. One of her closest friends landed in an emergency, which meant that she couldn't go on a blind date. To help her friend in need, Emma stepped in and went on a date instead. *Just doing a small favor* is what Emma originally thought until her eyes landed on a tall stranger at the cafe.

Both of them connected instantly as they discussed their respective lives. There was even a light moment when they laughed about doing their friends a favor by being on this blind date. After that, they started going on more dates while getting to know each other better, talking about their childhood, college days, and respective careers. Everything seemed to be fitting right, as if it was meant to be. A year went by quickly, where both of them enjoyed nights out and romantic getaways while being in each other's company.

One evening Noah took Emma on the most romantic candlelight dinner on the rooftop of a restaurant. Suddenly the lights went out, and it was pitch black. Emma couldn't even see Noah's face. Suddenly, fireworks lit up the sky, which caught Emma off guard as she was amazed at the wonderful sight. While Emma was busy watching the fireworks, she failed to notice Noah right by her side. He knelt on one knee, ready to pop the question which would forever change their lives. Of course, Emma cried and kept screaming "yes" as tears streamed down her face. They got married at Emma's family's farmhouse in spring and went on a romantic honeymoon.

Hitting the Bumpy Road

One year into their loving marriage, Noah and Emma started to witness some turbulence in their marriage. It all started with small fights about not giving enough time to each other and their differences in opinion that were a struggle to resolve. During the honeymoon phase, differences between two people usually are overshadowed by their overflowing love, so they overlook everything, including their partner's flaws. The real problems start surfacing only after the blooming period of love passes away. Sometimes, giving in to your partner's expectations or apologizing for the misunderstanding even when you weren't at fault is the easiest way to stop fighting. Still, all of it is a temporary solution.

Usually, when a nail wounds you, you can only heal it by disinfecting the wound and applying some ointment rather than kissing it. Problems within marriages are just the same, and they have to be addressed and accepted before you can find the solution. Although Noah and Emma were facing problems, they were not addressing these issues. In the heat of the moment, there would be a fight, and then the next moment, one of them would say sorry, or the other would try to understand their needs and give in to their partner's expectations. However, they would fail to address the big elephant in the room, which would lead to more problems in their marriage.

"Hitting the Bumpy Road" is exactly the phase where your marriage is starting to get stagnant, but the feeling is not persistent enough for you to address it. Usually, when couples start fighting in the early stages of their marriage, they believe that "fights are bound to happen. The only way to grow in a marriage is to learn through fights. After all, there is no love without a small fight." However, within a marriage, some fights help you address the problem head-on to find a solution, so they have a rather positive outcome. But some fights eventually lead to a breakdown and exhaustion. The only thing you crave is to escape when everything starts to fall apart. Our golden couple, Noah and Emma, faced the same crisis one day after a huge fight.

It All Falls Apart

Noah and Emma were already fighting on countless occasions, which meant less talking or listening and more screaming at the top of their voices, exclaiming how unsatisfied they were. Most of the time, Noah would be stuck at his workplace until late at night, which rarely left any space for them to get intimate or have a meaningful conversation. Emma would always be having the same overwhelming thoughts, like, *What am I even doing with this marriage? Noah barely says a word to me every day.* Emma finally decided that she needed to have "the talk" with Noah before it all went down the rabbit hole.

One evening Noah came home tired from the day's work after having a horrible meeting with his boss. All Noah wanted was to relax at home, sit in front of the TV, and watch his favorite show. But as soon as Noah entered the front door, Emma popped up, "Finally, you are back home. Why have you been working so late?" At that moment, Noah thought he would be better off at some club than being a victim of his wife's firing questions. He wished that his wife understood the situation and would just serve him some dinner before loading him with questions. "You know there has been a new project assigned to me, Emma. I have to finish it before the deadline."

At that point, Emma was frustrated and she blew up. "It would be nice if you could just come home a bit early instead and spend some quality time with me." Noah was frustrated about his sticky work situation, and to top that, Emma was wounding him by complaining about his shortcomings. Suddenly Noah got angry at his wife and said something unforgivable in a fit of rage, "Well who is going to provide the dinner at this table each day if I slack off at work and get fired for some reason? You should be grateful that I am at least trying to earn some money so that you can live the best life." Emma was shattered.

Never in a million years did Emma think that Noah would say something demeaning to her. "How can you say this to me?" Emma screamed. "I do everything in my power to keep this house and our marriage together." This was the breaking point in their marriage where she finally thought that everything had been done and dusted. The only thing that Emma wanted to do was leave because she was exhausted from frequent fights. Their marriage was slowly losing its magic, and she did not understand how to get through this. Like Emma, Noah was going through a rough patch with this entire situation. Noah thought, *If only I could turn back time and be with Emma when we first met.*

Just like the fate of our golden couple, many relationships and marriages have been suffering the erosion of time. Many couples break apart when all the loving feelings start to fade away. Instead of addressing their problems, they start to run away from the same problems. When Emma tried to address the elephant in the room, Noah just brushed it off with some mean words instead of trying to listen to her and get through the tough situation. Just like Emma and Noah, you may also be feeling hopeless at this very moment. "How do I build a healthy relationship with my spouse when all we do is argue and fight?" To help with this question, we have written this book. We hope it will help you reinvent your relationship through our seven-step guide and ultimately transform and heal your relationship from all the stress, fights, and distrust that has developed over time.

The Ultimate Guide for a Successful Relationship

Most relationship failures are linked to the fact that two people aren't aware of their problems and how they can face them together. As individuals, we always look at problems as something we have to face alone, but a relationship is about two people, which means you have to learn to do everything together. You have to learn to communicate, stand united, and fight against your issues. Most relationships don't address their issues until too late, and all these issues boil down to one problem: lack of communication. This is exactly why we wrote this book, because we are hoping you will address these issues and work on them with your partner. This book will be divided into a seven-step guide that will discuss various problems every couple faces and the various techniques you can use to overcome them. At the end of each chapter, we have inserted some application exercises to help you evaluate your feelings and become aware of the problems you face in your relationship.

Chapter 1 starts with basics and goes into a person's brain dynamics and traumatic experiences; how the male and the female brain are wired differently, and how a thinker behaves differently from a feeler. We will also touch upon the traumatic experiences of a person; how an abusive upbringing or a past relationship can become a hurdle in your relationship. Lastly, we will talk about rewiring your brain to overcome these problems and work together in your relationship.

Chapter 2 is all about the communication problems each couple faces. We will start by talking about the communication gap between each couple and how they can repair this, how the communication breakdown occurs, and the common triggers that lead to disagreements between partners.

In Chapter 3, we discuss how couples can effectively listen to each other, different ways they can ensure that they are being heard, how partners need to validate each other's feelings, and the secret ingredient that makes you a power couple.

In Chapter 4, we touch upon a person's emotional state and how it can affect relationships. We will essentially give you various calming techniques to overcome this state and talk about the power of the pause button that will help you when you are overwhelmed.

Chapter 5 talks about the concept of forgiveness—how important it is and why each partner should learn to forgive their significant other. We also discuss how forgiveness can lead to softening the heart and why the way you talk to your partner changes your relationship dynamics.

Chapter 6 is where we discuss the importance of trust, how broken trust can affect your marriage, and different ways you can rebuild your broken trust. We also discuss how checking in with your partner can strengthen your bond and help you build a healthy relationship.

Lastly, in Chapter 7, we discuss the outcomes of using all the techniques that we listed above and how our golden couple overcame their relationship problems using them.

Throughout this entire book, we have used different examples involving our golden couple and certain other instances to help you understand each problem. We have also offered different strategies that you can use to solve these issues through your effort, understanding, and empathy. All these techniques are guaranteed to help you in one form or other to heal your damaged relationship. Without any further ado, we will dive straight into Chapter 1, where we will talk about the biomechanics of the brain and traumatic experiences.

Chapter 1:

Step 1—Why Are We This Way?

Noah and Emma have been experiencing some turbulence in their relationship, creating a rift between them. Our once loving couple is now busy locking horns with each other, with neither of them ready to let go. Noah is tired of his surroundings and wants to have a relaxing evening, whereas Emma wants to spend some quality time with Noah and have a meaningful conversation. Instead, they have been busy throwing verbal jabs at one another while they continue to feel wounded.

Now the only question remaining is, why are we this way? Noah and Emma could have just openly communicated to each other and avoided this entire meltdown. Why is communication so difficult in a relationship? Let us understand through two factors: the biomechanics of our brains and the traumatic events of our past. When we talk about biomechanics of the brain, we will be touching upon the areas where male and female thinking leads to differences in the relationship. By having a thorough understanding of these differences, we will see how two people can resolve their differences and learn to understand each other.

On the other hand, touching upon past trauma will enable partners to understand how to deal with each situation more sensitively. Finally, when we talk about rewiring the brain, we will discuss certain techniques that can help you evaluate the situation and your partner before jumping the gun and getting into fights. Let us now move on and talk about the biomechanics of the brain.

How Does the Male Brain Differ From the Female Brain?

Our brains are known to perform a series of functions that assist us in our everyday lives. One of the most important areas where the brain helps us is communication and building relationships. A part of the brain known as the "frontal lobe" helps us with our cognitive abilities such as speech, memory, and expressions. Another part of the brain, called Broca's area, located on the left side, also helps convert our ideas into speech. Through all the neural connections, every human brain allows its host to conduct various activities, including communicating and expressing their feelings. So what is this difference between male and female brains here? Aren't all human brains the same? Let us get into the details to understand this better.

How Do Males and Females Behave Differently?

Although the human brain structure does not change based on gender, we will always find a difference of approach between the two. Males and females often share different perspectives about various things and approach situations differently. For instance, the majority of the males are thinkers, meaning they find a logical solution for every situation. If there is water leakage, they will use various plumbing tools and fix it. Suppose the television screen went blank due to some wiring problem; they will fix it. In short, males like to immediately find solutions to a problem to quickly resolve the situation at hand without leaving much space to feel anything.

On the other hand, female brains are slightly different because they are natural feelers. They love to listen to someone's problem; to be empathic and support them through encouraging words. If a female sees someone crying about their difficult situation, they will listen to them, pat their backs, and tell them that it's going to be okay. Females are natural listeners, which allows them to understand other people, help others, and nurture their growth. So you can see there are differences in approach between both genders, but what drives these differences? To understand this, let us go back and understand the fundamentals of the human brain structure.

Brain Wiring Among Males and Females

Brain wiring is simply a connection between neurons created by their axons. Axons are an extension of the neuron itself, so they connect with the oyster neurons and send signals while the human body performs various tasks. Neurons are the most important part of the body because they form a part of the nervous system, and at the same time, they keep sending signals to the brain so that it is aware of its surroundings. Now how does this affect the two genders?

According to an article written by Rob Pascale and Lou Primavera for *Psychology Today* back in April 2019, both the male and the female brains are wired a bit differently. The male brain is wired from the front portion to the backside on the left and the right hemispheres. A female brain is wired across the left and right hemispheres. These neurological differences between the two genders have led to differences between them, such as women being good at remembering the faces of different people. In contrast, men are good at remembering different things or situations. These wiring differences also affect both genders on a mental level. For instance, females tend to suffer from depression and stress a lot more than males, leading to nervous breakdowns and relationship problems. At the same time, men are more prone to developing dyslexia and autism, which affects their daily lives. Considering all these factors, we can understand why the coping mechanism of both genders is rather different.

Lastly, if we had to touch upon one more point, it would be about the emotional differences the genders experience due to neurological differences. If we consider females, we know that female counterparts show strong emotional reactions, especially during adverse situations, because they have a higher level of blood flow in the cingulate gyrus, a part of the brain that processes emotions. Males are usually calm and composed while dealing with adversity. They are looking for a logical way to use their "I will fix it" mentality, so they are not emotionally influenced easily. These are the most fundamental differences based on neurological brain structure that affect the way both genders behave in a relationship. To understand this deeper, let us discuss how the male and female behaviors differ when they are bonding with the opposite gender.

Men and Women in a Relationship

In his famous book, *Men Are From Mars, Women Are From Venus*, John Gray talks about how males and females are supposed to be different. In the first chapter of the book, John Gray clearly states how we are always at odds with the opposite sex because we are frustrated and expect them to be the same way we are. He quotes, "We desire them to want what we want and feel the way we feel." During most fights with the opposite gender, you will always find yourself in a situation where your male partner doesn't understand how you feel or the female partner says how their lovers fail to express themselves openly. We will cover these small communication gaps in the next chapter, where we will talk about communication breakdown.

Males and females have different ways of showing their love and expressing their feelings when they are in a relationship. For instance, Emma is very distressed about a certain situation in her life. She just had a fight with her mother over a call, and she is upset over the harsh exchange between them. She wants to talk about this with someone who will listen to and comfort her. As soon as Noah arrives home in the evening, he notices their house atmosphere is a little off. He finds Emma lying on the couch as if she were exhausted. Emma looks up to see Noah and tries to have a small talk. Emma tells Noah about having a bad day and her ugly fight with her mother during their talk. Instead of trying to understand Emma, Noah tells her, "Sweetie, you know she talks that way at times, you should ignore it. Maybe try overlooking it once in a while."

Now, if Noah were to say the same to another guy, he would have taken up his advice and followed through with it. However, Emma wasn't here trying to find a solution but rather needed some warm, comforting words, like, "I know this must have been difficult for you. It will be alright after a while." But what she got instead would make her feel more upset rather than at ease. Noah tried to find a solution for Emma, thinking this was a problem for her, instead of making her feel better about this difficult situation. This is commonly how most couples fight because there is a bit of misunderstanding due to the expectations and different approaches each has to resolve certain situations. We will discuss various techniques to help you understand these differences in the latter half of the book as we discuss rewiring the brain. Since we now finally understand the male and female brain biomechanics, let us go further and talk about how past experiences can also affect our relationships with our partners.

Upbringing and Past Trauma

In the beginning, when we are going out on dates and learning new things about our partner, it is truly exciting. We learn about their likes and dislikes, from favorite foods, color, and vacation spots to their pet peeves, habits, and more. However, during the beginning stages, the relationship is still developing, which means that we don't open up completely to our partner and talk about our emotions. This is also one of the reasons why the beginning phase of any relationship is the honeymoon phase, where partners are busy wooing each other while they giddily fall in love. The emotional baggage that they carry is always shadowed behind their smiles and happiness. Slowly as the relationship progresses, each partner learns something new about their partner. Sometimes we also learn about distressing situations our partner experienced during their childhood or while they were teenagers. For better understanding, we will divide this section into two parts. In the first, we talk about childhood trauma, and in the second, about past relationship trauma.

How Does Our Upbringing Affect Our Relationships?

Our upbringing plays a major part in our lives. It affects how we build our perspectives, relationships, and careers. Not all of us have happy memories of our childhood where our parents tucked us in and kissed us before we slept. Childhood trauma has become a major hindrance for young adults who constantly feel guilty and shameful due to the hardships they faced while they were young. Some of you have gone through certain traumatic events during your childhood, such as being abused physically, emotionally, and/or mentally. This could be an outcome of your parents going through similar circumstances during their own childhoods. Some of you have been brutally beaten by your parents as they flushed their angry emotions on you, while others were the victims of verbal abuses, including swearing and shouting, which is hurtful. Either way, childhood trauma has extreme effects on a person and their relationships. To understand this, we must understand the after-effects of childhood trauma on a person.

After-Effects of Childhood Trauma

Many children who suffer childhood trauma also suffer from mental health disorders. They develop a certain amount of anxiety and isolate themselves from other people. Losing any sense of attachment, most of them try to avoid bonding with other people or building relationships. Childhood trauma can have a huge impact on their personality development, which is also highlighted by their lack of confidence within themselves. The two main factors that are affected by this kind of trauma include:

- **Trust**—Any victim of childhood trauma often suffers from trust issues as they believe that other people will only bring them pain and suffering rather than any form of happiness. We all know what role trust plays in any relationship. Trust defines our loyalty toward relationships and brings us comfort in another person's company. If a person cannot trust you, they will find it hard to open up to you and be vulnerable in your company. Relationships require you to be an open book with your partner to build your trust and share certain things that only they are allowed to know. If partners cannot trust one another, there will always be a rift between them, leading to a fallout in later stages. Being in a relationship as a victim of childhood trauma can be an uncomfortable and scary experience.

- **Emotional intelligence**—Emotional intelligence, or EQ, measures the person's capacity to effectively understand and manage their own and other people's emotions. It helps people become aware of their feelings, which helps them regulate their emotions and express themselves better. In a relationship, EQ is a very important element. It helps partners remain empathic and allows them to express themselves while they understand each other's emotions freely. However, people who have suffered from childhood trauma develop some negative perspectives, especially in terms of emotions, which can affect their EQ to a certain extent.

If you look at both these factors, they are equally important from a relationship perspective. The absence of these two elements is usually found in victims who have suffered childhood trauma. Victims also tend to have poor relationships with their partners because trauma can be self-destructive, and people experience certain negative emotions while showcasing aggressive behavior. If you are in a relationship with a victim of childhood trauma, how does this affect you?

First and foremost, victims are always insecure about themselves. They have been told that they were not good enough after being abused or even relatively abandoned by their parents all their lives. As mentioned previously, this takes a certain emotional toll on your partner, as they lack self-confidence. Many studies have pointed out that victims of childhood trauma had poor relationships with their partners while showcasing high levels of insecure attachment. A study published by Pamela Cristobal and colleagues for NCBI back in 2017 found that survivors of childhood trauma would often experience insecure attachment in relationships due to physical negligence and emotional abuse during their childhood.

The second thing that you may come across is that the survivors of such trauma often display some form of toxic behavior. For instance, they may show passive behavior about certain situations and fail to express their needs clearly. Some of them may even show passive-aggressive behavior, or they may react aggressively during difficult circumstances, which can hurt the partner. Suppose you are in a relationship with a victim of childhood trauma. In that case, you may experience some turbulence in the later stages of the relationship when your partner finds it difficult to be vulnerable in your company and express their emotions. Either way, there are certain ways through which you can connect with your partner and override the aftermath of trauma.

Emotional Trauma From Previous Relationships

When we talk about past trauma in relationships, we mainly refer to the unresolved trauma a person experiences due to their past relationships. We all have been in relationships at one point, and while some may have been successful, others often fall apart, maybe due to a partner's toxic behavior, broken trust, or abuse. Not everyone shares a rosy relationship with their partner. While some of you may have been victims of some childhood trauma that leaves behind unresolved emotions, others are victims. They may have experienced the best of life, yet they fail to receive the required amount of love from their partner. This will leave a scar on their being, making them afraid to pursue a new, healthy relationship with the right partner.

Perhaps you have felt like this: *Oh, this person was right for me! I knew we were a perfect match, but for some reason they have been distant.* You know that person is the one for you, yet you can't reach out to them. The trauma from previous relationships gnaws your heart, and the wounds have failed to heal over time. In such scenarios, people try to avoid any form of relationship with another person and close themselves away from others. They are afraid that being with another person will result in a similar outcome and they will end up alone again. There are various reasons why your partner has developed trauma due to events in the past. Some of these factors will affect your current relationship with them. Let us look at some of the main reasons a relationship is affected due to past trauma.

- Your partner was either abused verbally or mentally in their previous relationship, making them afraid to open up to you. Many times during a fight, you may raise your voice so that your point gets across. This happens almost unknowingly, and it will hurt your partner, especially if they have been victims of verbal abuse in a past relationship.

- Your partner got cheated in their past relationship, making it extremely hard for them to trust you. At times, you may find them checking up on things to confirm your whereabouts and the things you do every day. Although lack of trust is a given, especially if a partner has been cheated on, at some point, this behavior can cause suffocation and create problems in a relationship.

- Abuse in a physical form often leaves a deep impression, and your partner may need a lot of time to recover. Many victims who have been brutally assaulted physically or sexually by their partner have difficulty being intimate with the right person. They are afraid that their partner will snap at any moment and cause them pain and suffering, so they particularly avoid any form of relationship, especially physical. Some of you may have experienced that your partner is especially distant when you try to become intimate with them, which may be due to some unhealed trauma that stops them from being vulnerable and pursuing an intimate relationship with their partner.

We can see that trauma leaves behind emotional wounds which can take time to heal. To support your partner through these difficult times, you must ensure that you support them by understanding their feelings, making it easier to communicate with them. You have to help them realize that they are in a safe space right now through this relationship with you. Lastly, through some trust exercises, you can strengthen your bond and help them see that you will always have their back no matter what. By using different techniques, you can connect with your partner and help them through this healing process. In the next section, we will talk about rewiring between the male and female brain and how a thinker can connect with a feeler.

Rewiring the Brain for Better Understanding and Effective Communication

In the previous two sections, we disclosed the secrets of how a male brain works differently from the female brain and how traumatic experiences through our upbringing and past relationships can cause your partner to behave differently in an unhealthy fashion. In this section, we will be discussing the different techniques that you can use to communicate with your partner, keeping in mind the differences in your thought process. Additionally, we will also talk about connecting with your partner when they have been a victim of past traumatic experiences.

How Do I Convey My Feelings?

We already saw in the biomechanics of the brain section how males and females behave differently from one another. The difference in thinking, perception, and how they perceive feelings can cause friction between a couple. With Noah and Emma, Noah has a habit of being quiet when he is troubled by something, while Emma likes to be loud and convey her feelings. In her book, *Appreciating People*, prominent psychologist and therapist Miriam Adahan categorizes people into two groups. One is a group of thinkers, and the other, a group of feelers. Thinkers tend to focus less on their emotions and usually have a logical perspective for every situation, whereas feelers are more expressive about their emotions. From what we saw, males usually fall under the thinking category; however, this does not necessarily rule out the females. Certain females do tend to think logically rather than being the emotional type. On the other hand, most females fall under the feeler category, and their empathic nature underlines that. Either way, the common heterosexual marriage is composed of a thinker (male) and a feeler (female), or vice versa.

When a thinker is in a relationship with a feeler, there are bound to be differences in opinion. For example, a thinker takes some time to understand their partner's emotional needs because they are too busy comprehending the situation logically. In the above section, Men and Women in Relationships, we see how Noah tries to dismiss Emma's feelings by simply telling her to ignore her mother's rants. Like Noah, many thinkers like to find the best solution to any problem without trying to understand how others feel. On the other hand, feelers have difficulty comprehending what a thinker is feeling. Thinkers are like closed books who rarely ever express themselves because of their lack of emotional needs. They don't exactly feel things too deeply and at times brush away emotions quickly by relying on their problem-solving ability. So how does a thinker connect with a feeler? Both of them can use numerous techniques to ensure that they create a safe space while trying to solve the problem together.

- **Carefully put forth your problem**—Every problem is accompanied by one common human emotion: frustration. We are irked by our troubles and lash out at our loved one or, in our case, our partner. If something is troubling you, it is always better to talk about your problems instead of feeling annoyed. Sometimes we bottle up our problems and then lash out at our partner, shouting at the top of our voices, stating that we have a problem. The first thing you can learn to do is figure out what is troubling you and then approach your partner, saying, "Hey, can we possibly talk? Something is troubling me lately." This way, you can lay all your cards on the table without causing any unnecessary conflict.

- **Stop with the accusations**—When you are angry, you are most likely to complain about your partner and accuse them of unusual behavior or habits. *All you do is care about yourself. You always think about yourself. The problem is you never understood me.* These are some of the most basic things you must have told your partner at least once. Here is the difference: When a female accuses the male of not understanding or being helpful, it disappoints them. It makes them feel weak, scared, and helpless, like they are not good enough for their partner. Most of the time, what we feel is temporary; for instance, our partner not being understanding may be due to a lack of clarity which can be resolved through conversation. Instead of accusing our partners, we just let them know where they went wrong. Let us stop pointing fingers and make peace through meaningful conversations.

- **Empathize with them**—It is natural for women to sympathize with others and relate to their emotions due to their empathic nature. However, males have a huge problem in the same area. When listening to someone's problems, they are too busy thinking of a way out rather than empathizing with their emotions. That is why many females are seen complaining about their male partners not listening to them or understanding their emotions. It isn't exactly a problem but rather two different perspectives. When a female is talking about her problems, a male can embrace her and tell her, "I understand that this must be tough for you, but it is going to be okay." By doing this, females feel a bit encouraged, and they know that they will always have a shoulder to cry on and rely on at any point.

- **Create a positive environment**—Most of the time, partners fight with each other because they have created a negative space that often destroys their relationship. Anyone would get easily irritated or disappointed when the first thing they hear is their partner's nagging rather than warm words like "Welcome home." To change this, both males and females need to understand their partner's needs and create a positive environment. For instance, females can do something known as victory talks to encourage their male partners by talking about their kids' growth, their healthy routine, and the good things about their day, which makes a male feel more welcomed than complaints asking them to fix problems. On the other hand, males can try to be more open and honest about their thoughts by sharing them with female partners, making them feel that they have earned their partner's trust.

All in all, these techniques will help you build a deep and meaningful relationship with your partner and even strengthen your connection. In the initial stages of the relationship, many partners don't make much effort to repair rifts, using the logic that their other half will get over it with time, but the reality differs. Partners can develop a grudge over small things, which creates problems in the long term. By understanding your partner and their thought process, you can build a strong connection and learn to tackle difficult situations by facing them together.

Every relationship has its challenges that can weigh down on partners, but only through clear means of communication and understanding can both overcome these hurdles. With time, patience, love, understanding, and building trust, you will strengthen the relationship with your partner. In the end, communication is always the key to building a healthy relationship. After a thorough understanding of how the brain and past experiences affect our relationships, in the next chapter, let us understand how communication gaps exist in relationships and how we can solve them.

Key Takeaways

- Due to the differences in the male and female brain wiring, both have different perspectives, thoughts, and behavior. Understand these differences and communicate with your partners to create an everlasting bond.

- Trauma victims have unhealed emotional wounds which can affect your relationship. You can help them heal by supporting them through moral encouragement and developing a safe space in the relationship.

- Every relationship has challenges in one form, and the only way partners can overcome these challenges is by being united through clear communication.

Application Workbook 1

Are You a Thinker or a Feeler?

The clash between male and female brains is often associated with the way each of them behaves. We have highlighted these differences, but how do we identify them? Go through this short application exercise and note down your answers to evaluate your personality. Try to answer these as truthfully as possible to determine your type.

While having a tough conversation with your partner, would you rather focus on...

- The subject matter; i.e., what the other person is telling you?
- The tone of the person; i.e., how the other person is talking about the issue?

What is the most important thing for you?

- Being compassionate toward others regardless of what they do.
- Having fair judgment before you pursue that person.

If a person had to impress you, what should they do?

- Talk about some logical things that blow your mind.
- Have an emotional appeal by displaying some empathy.

Which prominent historical figure do you admire the most?

- Mother Teresa
- Albert Einstein

Which personality traits suit you the best?

- Being emotional, displaying compassion, and having empathy.
- Being blunt, making judgments, and thinking logically.

If you had to become a mirror and show someone that they are wrong, you would...

- Just tell it straight to their face without any hesitation.
- Try to tactfully tell them about their wrongdoings without being harsh.

Based on the answers to all the above questions, you can determine whether you are a thinker or a feeler.

Journaling About Trauma Response

We will be dividing these exercises into two parts, and each of these will have a series of questions which you can answer with a yes or a no. The first one will address the victim and the second will be addressing their partner. Each of them can use this exercise to understand their relationship and overcome any obstacles.

Addressing the Trauma Victim

Answer all the questions listed below with a yes or a no:

- Have you been having a hard time trusting your partner?
- Do you feel insecure in this relationship?
- Is your current relationship being affected due to your abusive upbringing/past relationship?
- Has your partner ever displayed any abusive behavior toward you?
- Do you feel fulfilled and satisfied in this relationship?

Based on your answers, you will be able to evaluate your feelings and the status of your relationship. If the majority of your answers tilt toward a yes, you will have to break down whether you are experiencing problems because you are holding back from your partner or because your relationship is simply toxic. Either way this should give you a clear picture of your relationship.

Addressing the Victim's Partner

- Has your partner been distant lately?
- Have you ever raised your voice or displayed any form of abusive behavior toward your partner?
- Are you able to be an emotional support for your partner?
- Has your partner opened up to you about their trauma experience?
- Do you feel fulfilled and satisfied in this relationship?

The partner will mainly take this test to determine the health of their relationship. Most partners are completely unaware of their significant other's traumatic experiences until later in a relationship. If the majority of your answers tilt toward a no, it is time for you to communicate with your partner so that you can understand them better.

Chapter 2:

Step 2—The Communication Gap

Emma and Noah were once a loving couple who would never hesitate to open up to each other and talk about different things. Previously we saw how Noah and Emma fell in love and always communicated their feelings with each other, then something went wrong with their relationship. When the beginning phase of any relationship is blooming, everything is still new and different. Couples are just starting to get comfortable around one another and make every effort to create a strong bond between them. The more time you spend with each other, the more you get comfortable, and that is when each starts revealing their true self. You start being more honest, vulnerable, and emotional in front of your partner, showing how much you trust them.

However, in the previous chapter, we saw how recalling past events could affect the brain and communication between two people. Similarly, most of the time, the communication gap is usually an outcome of unusual circumstances. Your partner is under stress or going through a hard time, but they are doing their best to put up a smile and be there for you. Most of us try to hide our problems behind the curtain, building up our emotions by overthinking everything until finally, we have a big fight and the entire show goes down.

The same thing happened with Noah and Emma, but he never revealed he had a big project ongoing at work, and Emma never tried to tell Noah how she felt. This was simply a small communication gap that would lead to fights and create problems in their relationship over time. In this chapter, we will discuss the problem with the communication gap in relationships, the reasons for communication breakdown, the key triggers that lead to such a gap, and how we can resolve this using some techniques.

How Big Is the Problem?

A communication gap usually occurs when one partner's words are understood differently by the other. For instance, Emma is upset about something, but she decides to put up a facade instead of talking to Noah. Emma laughs at all his jokes at the dinner table while she feels uneasy within and watches a movie with Noah in her deflated mood. When they finally go to bed, Noah is thinking, Today was a great day! But Emma is still silently suffering. So what is the problem here? Emma was upset, but her actions indicated otherwise, and Noah never knew whether she was upset in the first place. Everything went quite well from Noah's perspective, from a romantic dinner to their late movie night. To get a clearer picture, we already know how the communication gap occurred between the two partners.

There are usually three stages that lead to a communication gap between partners. Just like every problem, it all starts with small things that later become big, and the frustration of dealing with it time and again sets you off. With each stage, the communication gap only widens and damages the relationship that you share with your partner. Let us try to understand these three stages to see how the communication gap occurs.

Stage 1—Too Busy Overthinking to Express Your Feelings

This may seem like something only teenagers do, but believe me, adults tend to overthink things, especially sensitive ones. The overthinking tendency often shuts us off from the world and leaves us helpless. Worrying about the smallest thing yet not expressing yourself will make you feel overwhelmed and strain your relationship. Take this, for instance: Noah made a small mistake at his workplace, which led to a huge outburst with his boss.

Noah has always been the perfectionist who rarely makes a mistake, even a small one. He was quite bothered by the whole office drama and kept to himself most days. We tend to distance ourselves from loved ones when we are under stress or worried about something. Emma kept thinking, Noah comes home late often nowadays and doesn't even talk much when he is home. However, Emma doesn't want to overthink this, and she decides to prepare a delicious meal for Noah and make him feel at home.

The next day, Noah is again late to reach home, but instead, Emma greets him at the door. Looking at Emma's smiling face, Noah is once again feeling guilty about being away from her all this time, but he smiles. Emma scoops him in her arms and hugs him tightly. While hugging him, she notices a sweet smell coming from his shirt. *Perhaps a lady's perfume? Is that why Noah is usually coming home late?* Emma is shattered. She feels that Noah has been coming home late and keeping his distance from her because he is doing something behind her back.

Now there is a communication gap here, as you can see. First of all, Noah has been unintentionally keeping his distance because he is too busy worrying about his problems. Emma was kept in the dark all this time, leading her to assume the worst-case scenario instead of talking it out with her partner. If only Noah had expressed himself after settling down and telling Emma about his problems while she did the same in return, neither would feel this way, and there wouldn't be a communication gap in their relationship. This is the most common and basic stage where partners often distance themselves while in their "overthinking persona." When and how to get through this stage is something we will be discussing in the next section.

Stage 2—Being Defensive With "I Am Always Right" Attitude

Some partners are rebellious and always like to fight over the smallest things, leading to tons of arguments. When you are fighting, they will often become defensive and disregard your point of view, which can put you off and make you feel disrespected. This leads to our second stage of communication gap, where a person is so busy proving themselves right that they forget to understand the other person's perspective.

Let's try to understand this from Noah's and Emma's points of view. The couple was having a basic discussion about buying a new house since their old house was starting to feel cramped, with Emma already seven months pregnant and baby on the way. Emma wanted a big house with some extra rooms, a backyard, front porch, a spacious kitchen, a study room, and the list goes on. Noah has always dreamed of getting a big home, too, but he didn't feel the need to buy an extra spacious home like Emma imagined. With his current pay, it would take him eons to finally pay off the mortgage if he were to buy such an extravagant space, but Emma disagreed with the whole thing.

She expressed her desires to Noah, stating, "At some point, we will have three kids who will be running around the house. Plus, extra rooms are always beneficial for having guests over. Your brother has always been keen on visiting us with Michelle and the kids. Wouldn't it be better to buy a spacious place with some comfort and warmth?" Noah understood Emma's perspective, but he told her, "Em, love, I understand where you are coming from, but trust me, sweetheart, there is absolutely no need to buy a gigantic house which would fit in an elephant. We can notch it down a bit and still be able to accommodate everyone, including our kids and guests."

Emma was getting a bit agitated. She knew she was right, but her husband wasn't ready to listen to her. "No, Noah, you don't understand. We do need a big house after all. I am tired of living in a small space that is all cramped up. Will you please listen to me for once?" She was too busy being defensive and barely paid any heed to Noah's rational explanation on this issue. By always wanting to be right about something, partners avoid listening to what their significant other has to say, which leads to gaps in their communication and their relationship.

Stage 3—Shutting Down All Means of Communication

This may be regarded as the most toxic stage of communication—when your partner refuses to communicate any problems while your relationship is falling apart. It just so happens that when people are feeling anxious or depressed about a certain matter, sometimes they choose to hide and never talk about it. Let us try to understand this through an example with our golden couple.

Emma's father, Jack, suffered from 'glioblastoma,' a stage four tumor leading to brain cancer. Jack had always been fond of his daughter, as they shared a close bond. Emma spent her entire childhood doing various activities with her father, be it fishing in the lake close to their farmhouse, telling ghost stories on camp nights, or listening to their favorite song, "Bohemian Rhapsody" by Queen, and dancing together to celebrate life.

His sudden death caused her grief and overwhelmed her with negative emotions. Emma only came to know about her dad's cancer a week before he passed away when her mother called her requesting that she come home. After spending a week together cherishing all the memories of her life, Jack passed away, and Emma couldn't stop crying. *You were my hero, Dad, and I wish we had more time.* Her father passing away made Emma feel lonely and depressed. She kept thinking about who will support her during the most difficult times and cheer her up. Noah gave Emma some space to process this uncertain situation for a few days. When Noah tried talking to Emma after some time, she would nod her head without saying anything.

Emma had shut down the entire communication system from her side while she grieved for her father. What Emma didn't know was that Noah was worried about her. The days she slept on her father's chair at night, Noah would carry her to the room and tuck her in the bed. When Noah heard sniffling noises in the bathroom, he would stand outside the door in case Emma needed anything. She would often skip her meals, and as her partner, he would try to coax her so that she wouldn't fall ill due to a weakened immune system.

Overlooking all these factors, Emma didn't see her partner's effort and still kept silent from her end. Although Noah was patient, he soon became frustrated and upset with this whole situation. Of course, he wanted Emma to have her own space and open up when she was comfortable, but he feared all his efforts were in vain. Emma didn't say a word to him. One day, Noah approached Emma. "Hey Em, I know you are not feeling okay, but I am here for you. I know this is hard for you, but please talk to me once. I am not trying to force you or anything, but I want to support you during such tough times."

Emma didn't say anything again, and Noah felt like he had been talking to a brick wall all this time. He wanted to fight with her, tell her *I am right here, Em!*, but he couldn't. Finally, Noah decided that it was better to leave before he lost control over his emotions and started fighting with Emma. Often when our partner shuts down communication from their end, it can be distressing because we cannot figure out their thoughts. This particular stage affects most relationships, especially if your partner has been a trauma victim. They will shut themselves out to avoid any painful experience.

Each of these stages can create a strain or damage your relationship. Communication is the main source that allows you to understand your partner's perspective while avoiding conflicts. When there is a gap in the main engine, it will either stop working efficiently or not work at all. This gap also affects relationships, which can create rifts or lead to separation if not resolved soon. To help you bury this hatchet, we will be discussing some techniques in the next section.

How Do I Connect With My Partner?

Since we have already gone through the three stages, the next thing you must be wondering about is *How do I get through this?* Any stage of communication gap leaves a great deal of strain on you, emotionally and mentally, which is exhausting. When partners get tired of each other, their relationship suffers greatly; however, there are ways to close down this communication gap and reconnect with your partner, which we will discuss in this section.

Express Yourself to Stop Overthinking

As we have previously expressed, overthinking is one of the major problems that leads to communication gaps in relationships. When a person is too busy living in their head, they often make up lies that make them uncomfortable and insecure. The best way to overcome this is by expressing your true feelings. By opening up with your partner and sharing your problems with them, you can easily overcome the first stage of the communication gap. Of course, this does not happen easily sometimes; it takes some time to share how we are truly feeling, but it is always better to openly express your feelings than to bottle them up and create misunderstandings.

Welcome Your Partner's Thought Process

In the second stage, we saw how heated the entire argument between Noah and Emma became just because the latter did not wish to compromise. After a cooldown period and some space, Emma realized that Noah was right all along. Being defensive is the most psychological way to express dislike toward a particular thing or when things are not going your way. However, in a relationship, two people have to learn to accept their partner's perspective rather than forcing their views. The second stage of the communication gap can damage your relationship with your partner and even lead to a fallout. The best way to close this gap is by listening to your partner's views, taking your time to understand them, and lastly, trying to establish a common ground on the issue rather than rooting for the "I am always right" cause.

Opening Up for Better Understanding

There are two types of people in this world—those who openly express their distaste for certain things and others who like to hide their pain behind their secret walls. This isn't a typical cliché but a reality. Emma fell into the second category when she decided to shut herself down while she grieved her father's loss. With Emma suddenly shutting down all forms of communication, Noah was confused and upset. He understood what Emma was going through but failed to comprehend their current situation. One fine day, Noah similarly approached Emma as he always did, but he was rather annoyed; however, he decided to be calm about this. Emma wasn't ready to open up, so Noah decided to leave her alone. Just as Noah was about to leave the house, Emma hugged him and started crying. Noah held her while she kept crying in his arms. After a few minutes, when Emma stopped crying, Noah asked her, "Are you feeling okay?" Emma shook her head from side to side, trying to tell him she wasn't okay.

Emma was finally showing some communication signs, so Noah didn't try to push her. He just held her in his arms. Sometime later, Emma spoke. "I thought I was strong enough to let Dad go. I feel so weak, Noah. I felt so lonely, and I wanted to talk, but I just didn't know how to tell you all these things I felt on the inside. I am so sorry." Noah tightly scooped Emma in his arms and told her that it was okay. "It is okay to feel this way, Em. Sometimes when we lose something precious, it leaves us feeling empty and uncertain. I know you shared a special bond with your father. I am sure he is watching over us now and he wouldn't want us to feel this way. It'll take some time, Emma, but I know you are strong and we can get through this together."

So there are two lessons we learn here. The first is that by displaying empathy and understanding, Noah was able to win Emma's trust and help her express her emotions. The next thing we see is that Emma learned an important lesson about opening up to her partner. When we are going through a tough time, we often shut down our communication system, letting our partner know that we don't wish to communicate when the reality is exactly opposite. This is when we need their support the most, but our actions say the opposite thing.

In a relationship, it is always better for two people to openly talk about their struggles so that each of them can understand and support their partner rather than one of them feeling exhausted. At the same time, the other one remains in the dark hole of uncertainty. Through some of these techniques, you can overcome the communication gap in your relationship. After understanding the three stages of the communication gap, it is important to go a bit deeper and understand how the communication breakdown occurs.

What Leads to a Communication Breakdown?

Communication is of great significance because by talking, you can solve problems, understand another person's perspective, and clear any misunderstandings. It is one of the great techniques that work well on a two-way street. Problems arise when there is a communication breakdown, be it in a business environment or a marriage. Communication breakdown is one of the biggest reasons why most marriages fall apart.

Just take the example of Emma and Noah from the introduction. After all this while, Emma decided to hold back on her communication only to have an emotional breakdown while fighting with Noah. On the other hand, Noah didn't want to make any efforts to talk with Emma, which blew things out of proportion. Would communication between the two of them change anything about the situation? Absolutely. Did they decide to make any changes to it? Not really.

Like Noah and Emma, most relationships suffer from communication breakdowns that often lead to misunderstanding and separation. To avoid making these mistakes, let us look at some common communication mistakes that can create a rift in your marriage.

Assuming the Worst-Case Scenario

It is human nature to have negative assumptions about various situations, especially when things go wrong. Any change in your life will lead to uncertainty, which may cause you to assume things. Relationships are not immune to assumptions, and many times, rifts within the relationship start with assuming the worst-case scenario. After the honeymoon phase in your relationship, things will start to change; your partner's behavior might change or your priorities will change, which will cause changes in your daily routine as well. It will be unsettling, and beyond a point, your brain starts getting crowded with unwanted assumptions.

For example, Noah is always on duty to take out the trash every morning before heading to work; however, he forgot to do it twice this week. Another time, Noah forgot to buy some groceries that Emma requested him to get on his way home from work. Emma started to wonder, *Is Noah running away from his responsibilities?* It all started with those small things, where Noah would overlook his responsibilities and not think much about them. It bothered Emma, who assumed that Noah didn't care much about her or respect her.

Now Emma had a problem, but instead of discussing this issue with Noah, she decided to keep assuming all the bad things, which eventually led to a rift between them. Emma would keep thinking, *Does he even care anymore? Why is Noah behaving this way?* Eventually, Emma would keep her distance from Noah and assume the worst-case scenario where she only felt uncomfortable and insecure. Even when Noah tried to talk to Emma, she would avoid him, often leading to fights. Without understanding the situation, we tend to create more problems instead of solving them by making negative assumptions. So, the first step to avoiding communication breakdown is to avoid making assumptions regarding your problems.

Avoiding Clear Means of Communication

Most of us are guilty of wanting our partners to read our minds and figure out the problem instead of telling them how we are feeling. Your partner isn't exactly Professor X from *X-Men*, who will instantly read your mind and make you feel better. This is exactly why communication was invented, and it is especially vital in relationships. Communication enables us to seek out problems, understand them, and solve them. Without communicating your problems with your partner, you will never be able to find a solution. During the happy phase of our relationships, our communication is strong. We tell our partner the smallest details at the beginning of the relationship, which slowly fade from memory in later stages.

After being in a relationship for a long time, partners feel embarrassed to share their problems or assume that their significant other knows how they are feeling. The problem is that your partner does not know what exactly you are going through. The only way they can understand you is through a clear communication method. Let us understand this through the example of Emma and Noah. Today, Emma had a horrible day. It all started with her having to take responsibility for a mistake her colleague made. Then she missed her last train home, which meant she would be late for her date night with Noah. When she finally made it back, Noah was sitting on the couch, busy watching a football match without any bother for their evening together.

Emma was upset, but instead of talking to Noah about it, she decided to keep it to herself. To begin with, she told Noah, "Hey, let's order some takeout since it's already late." Noah only thought *Emma must be tired, so we might as well stay at home.* While having dinner, Emma gave Noah subtle hints as she barely made any conversation and avoided eye contact. Noah asked Emma, "Are you alright, Emma? You seem to have spaced out there?" *Spaced out? I am upset, Noah!* That's what Emma said in her mind instead of saying it aloud. Finally, it was time to do the dishes, and today was Noah's turn; instead, he asked Emma to do it since he needed to finish some office work.

Emma had had enough of this and started shouting. "Noah, why can't you do anything right? Firstly, today I had to take responsibility for something which wasn't even my fault. Secondly, I missed our date night thanks to the sticky work situation, and finally, when I got home thinking that my husband will help me feel better, I saw you lying on the couch enjoying the game while I had an unpleasant day. Of course, I am not alright. Did you see me acting all cheerful while we had an indoor date with some cheap takeout?"

Noah was in shock for a minute as he didn't expect Emma to blow up. He was enraged by her behavior. After all, he had to cancel all the date plans because she was late. He said, "Cheap takeout? Emma, I don't understand what was so bad about having dinner at home. Plus, weren't you the one who called for it? It just so happened that we both had some things come up. You never told me that you were upset even when I asked you at the dinner table. I don't know why you are making such a big fuss." Emma, who was frustrated at this point, said, "Big fuss? Noah, I am tired and angry. We haven't gone out in such a long time and today would have been a great opportunity which was taken away by this unseen calamity." Noah started to understand Emma's situation and said, "I am not a mind-reader, Emma, and I can't figure out what you are feeling. You need to openly communicate your feelings with me so I can understand what you're going through. We will have plenty of date nights, so please don't be upset about this right now." Emma finally understood where she went wrong and decided to communicate with Noah whatever she felt.

What Emma did is something most of us do because we want our partner to act like a superhero and save the day. *Why can't my partner understand what I am feeling?* It is something most of us think about on our gloomy days. But how is your partner supposed to understand anything if you don't speak up? Failure to lay down your thoughts before your partner is another reason people experience communication breakdowns in relationships.

Playing the Blame Game

Arguments are part and parcel of any relationship, and they will occur more times than you can count. Some days will be the happiest in your relationship, while others will be the days you go head-to-head with your partner, fighting about minor issues or things that affect you. While fighting isn't necessarily grave, it can crack your relationship in certain cases. During an argument, it is only natural to pick at your partner, stating where they went wrong so that you can help them realize their mistakes. The real problem occurs when one person starts blaming the other for everything going wrong in their relationship.

For instance, Emma has been particularly engaged at her workplace since this year's recruiting season. She has been working overtime to ensure that the schedule of every recruit is structured well. While her performance at work is applauded, she has been neglecting her household chores and responsibilities for quite some time. Noah began to notice that Emma hadn't been spending quality time with him, taking their dog out for a walk, or even stocking up their refrigerator. Noah woke up this morning to realize that their milk carton was empty and there was no new carton left in the refrigerator.

Noah was extremely frustrated as this had been going on for a week. As soon as Emma arrived to prepare her morning coffee, she noticed that the milk carton was empty. "Hey Noah, are all the milk cartons already finished?" she asked. Noah, who was bubbling with anger, responded, "Well, Emma, someone forgot to stock up the refrigerator just like how they forgot to take our lovely Suzie for their walk."

Emma clicked her tongue as she realized that she had forgotten to go grocery shopping this week. "Noah, I am sorry, it really slipped me. I have been a bit busy this week." Noah was fuming by this point without knowing what Emma was going through all week. Frustrated, Noah said, "Emma you have not been doing anything the entire week. You barely did the dishes, never took Suzie for the walk, and even forgot grocery shopping. You have been neglecting your responsibilities and just focusing on everything related to your work. I go to work and I have been doing just fine while taking care of the house."

Emma was sad that Noah didn't see how hard she had been working all week. She barely had any stamina left, yet she did some dishes and even tried to clean up the mess around the house while she fed Suzie. In this situation, Noah blamed Emma for skipping out on her duties without understanding what she was going through. Sometimes it is always better to discuss the rough patches of your relationship with your partner before blaming them for running away or neglecting responsibilities. Playing the blame game with your partner is the third way communication breaks down in a relationship.

Giving Passive-Aggressive Responses

Some of us don't like to communicate our problems because we will instantly solve them. In relationships, some partners often take some time to express their displeasure regarding a particular circumstance. While it is okay to take some time before expressing our problems, some of us like to display passive-aggressive behavior to communicate our displeasure.

For instance, Noah and Emma went together to an office gathering organized by Emma's boss. While introducing Noah, one of Emma's colleagues named Julia had been clingy toward Noah and would spare no opportunity to flirt with him. While Noah would either give her straight answers or cut her off, Emma had been feeling envious. Noah knew that Emma wasn't feeling good, and he pulled away from the conversation in the most polite manner. He took Emma to one of the corners and asked her if she was okay. Emma constantly gave a fake smile and said that she was fine while she felt burning rage inside.

During their entire time together, Emma kept giving Noah the cold shoulder. When they finally left the party, Emma wouldn't even attempt to talk with Noah regarding her feelings. Noah finally broke the awkward silence in the car and asked Emma, "Hey Em, you have been awfully silent the entire ride. Is everything okay?" Emma started shouting, "Everything is fine, Noah. Why do you keep bugging me with this?"

"Emma, I know everything isn't fine. I know you are upset about how Julia was behaving, but you saw that I kept my distance." Emma finally blew up and said, "Julia? So you are now on a first-name basis with her? She has been eyeing you all night and what is frustrating is that you kept talking to her regardless."

Emma displayed passive-aggressive behavior right there when she finally told Noah how she felt in the end. Passive-aggressive behavior can be destructive in any relationship and should be avoided at all cost. We all are guilty of displaying such behavior at some point when we are upset, but it is always better to avoid it in any given occasion. Such behavior is one of the common causes of communication breakdown in relationships.

Other than these, the various other reasons that lead to a communication failure include not listening to your partner's problems, raising your voice while arguing, pinpointing their flaws, not sharing important life events with your partner, and breaching their trust. All these issues listed above may at some point cause your marriage to go upside down and be one step away from breaking apart. But this doesn't mean that there is no solution to the problem. Here are some of the techniques you can use to improve your communication with your partner, which may ultimately heal the relationship.

- **Listen carefully**—No matter how often you feel like cutting your partner off in the middle of the conversation to help them realize that you have a solution to their problem, listen attentively. Listen to how they are feeling, why they feel this way, and how this situation affects them. Most partners want their problems to be heard and seldom want a quick fix for the overall situation. By listening to them, you will help them unload their worries, and later you will be able to make them feel better through comforting words.

- **Be honest**—If you are going through some problem, be honest with your partner because you owe that much to them. Your partner isn't just going to be with you to make some happy memories. They will cherish you and support you during the hard times and stand beside you while you battle your demons. By being honest with them, you let them know that you trust them. Sometimes, honesty helps you convey your feelings better than displaying passive-aggressive behavior or bottling them up within you. So, it would help if you tried to be as honest as you possibly can be with your partner.

- **Pay attention**—In the world of social media, it is easy to get influenced by smartphones. We are busy scrolling through the phone during most of our free time rather than paying attention to our surroundings. The same can be true when you are dealing with your partner. Many of us are guilty of scrolling through our phones while our partner waits to spend some quality time with us. Next time, please do yourself a favor and switch your phone to silent mode, keep it aside, and give your partner the undivided attention they deserve.

- **Express gratitude**—How often have you told your partner about how grateful you are for their presence in your life? Just because our partners are beside us every day, we often take their presence for granted. One form of improving your communication with your partner is by expressing gratitude. Next time you see your partner preparing a meal, taking out the trash, playing with the kids, or taking your dog for a walk, just let them know how thankful you are. Expressing your gratitude through the words "thank you" will not only make their day but also put a bright smile on your face.

We have already touched upon various actions that lead to communication breakdown and simple techniques that will help you resolve this problem. Moving on to the next section of this chapter, we will talk about the common triggers that can lead to disagreement between partners and how you can resolve them.

What Are the Common Triggers That Lead to Relationship Disagreements?

Fighting with your partner isn't something that turns up out of thin air. Relationship disagreements are a byproduct of different key areas which can trigger a person and lead to an emotional reaction. Take this, for example: if a close friend of yours lied to you regarding their personal life, it would make you angry, and both of you would fight over this small misunderstanding. In relationships, certain key areas are very sensitive and can trigger a reaction from your partner. This reaction can cause a major fight between two people, which can cause irreparable damage. To avoid hurting your partner while dealing with these sensitive issues, let us understand the common triggers that start fights between partners and the different ways you can resolve them.

Money or Financial Support

In a world where inflation is continuously increasing, money is one of the most common topics that leads to an argument. Money forms the most important part of the discussion in any relationship because you have to plan and invest for your future and your kids. Many couples end up fighting when one keeps spending by shopping and buying takeout while the other is doing their best to save for their bright future. Other areas where you may fight involve the financial budget and personal investments.

Kid or an Additional Member

The number one fight between couples is whether or not they want kids. Many couples want to have children while they grow with their partner, and children can also cause a healthy relationship to bloom. However, many people do not want children, so even when one of the partners wants a child, they might disagree, which can be the starting point of a relationship breakdown. The next problem comes when a couple decides that they will have children but then argue about how the child should be born. If your partner has some fertility problem, your fight may consist of pursuing an advanced fertility treatment or surrogacy. Lastly, even after children are born, there are disagreements to be had between partners about their upbringing, ideologies, and perspectives that can crack a relationship and often lead to separation.

Quality Time and Romance

Each partner has their likes and dislikes, and these may cause conflicts between partners in a relationship. For instance, one of you enjoys some quiet time with your partner while you lay around and have a deep conversation while the other person likes watching a movie with you. This also leads to disagreements between the partners where they blame each other and point fingers at one another, stating, "You never want to spend some alone time with me." "You never like to watch my favorite movie with me." On the other hand, romance is quite a sensitive topic. As we previously mentioned, once the honeymoon phase ends, couples start to feel insecure and worried that they can't connect with their partner. It's yet another area that leads to couple fights and arguments that may eventually cause a rift instead of helping to strengthen their bond.

The In-Laws Conflict

Although you may build your own home and live with your partner and your kids, parents play a vital role in relationship dynamics. Some of you may not gel well with your in-laws, which can create a conflict where your partner will accuse you of not putting in enough effort. Other times, you may argue about when to visit the in-laws and how many times a year. Additionally, Christmas and Thanksgiving family dinner gatherings are always a common topic when couples argue. In other words, parents are another sensitive topic that can trigger your partner and lead to a difference of opinion.

Other common areas where partners fight with each other include household chores, pet peeves, and the feeling of envy. Each of these areas is sensitive to your partner, and the only way you can resolve any conflict is by approaching these issues with caution and communicating with your partner. To help you with this, let us go through some of the techniques to resolve these disagreements between partners.

- **Learn to talk it out**—Always ensure that you are trying to communicate your issues to your partner. For example, if you don't wish to indulge in any love-making process tonight, politely decline your partner's advances by letting them know that you are not in the mood. At the same time, never shame your partner for wanting more physical attention in your relationship. This way, both parties can learn to respect each other's perspectives while peacefully enjoying the process.

- **Plan everything together**—You can always plan things with your partner to stay ahead of the curve and ensure fewer conflicts arise in numerous situations. If it is anything important related to money or kids, you can always plan your monthly budget with your partner or discuss the right time to have children. Through this technique, both partners will realize that they are together on common ground, and there won't be any space for a surprise event.

- **Compromise for them**—When I say compromise, I don't mean compromise your choices but rather the way both of you do things together. As discussed, one partner loves deep conversation while the other loves watching movies as a form of quality time. In such cases, both can come to an agreement. Each of them can do something of their liking on alternate days and compromise while also spending quality time with one another and being happy. This way, you can also learn to enjoy what your partner does; for instance, laughing together while watching a funny movie or reminiscing about the time when you first fell in love. It also gives you insight into what your partner enjoys doing and enables you to understand them better.

Besides this, you can always discuss things before taking any action, like holiday planning. You can always discuss in advance whose parents you will be visiting this year for Christmas or even plan to have two separate celebratory dinners for each occasion, like one for Thanksgiving and the other for Christmas. This way, you avoid being selfish with one another and can still enjoy the warm holiday spirit with your family.

These are some techniques that you can use to repair your relationship with your partner and avoid fighting in an unproductive way. Remember that occasional fights in a relationship are inevitable. You may end up fighting with each other on many such topics, but you will learn to communicate, grow, and develop an understanding which will help you strengthen your relationship using these techniques.

We have already discussed two main areas: brain rewiring and the communication gap. In the next chapter, we will be discussing different ways partners can effectively learn to listen to each other while validating their emotions.

Key Takeaways

- Communication gaps can damage your relationship. To overcome these gaps, you must express yourself, consider their opinion, and open up to them in your relationship.

- Communication breakdown is a result of one partner trying to avoid their feelings instead of expressing their displeasure. You can overcome this by being patient and expressing your emotions to your partner.

- Common relationship triggers occur around most sensitive topics, which can be hard to address. To avoid conflicts, approach it carefully, talk politely, and understand where your partner is coming from before you start fighting with them.

Application Workbook—2

Self-Evaluation Survey

Through this short survey, we will be evaluating the health of your communication and what triggers you the most. Both of these will help you become self-aware about your behavior and to understand where you are going wrong so that you can improve in the future.

Breaking Down Communication

Here are some of the questions you must answer in your workbook so that you can go back and reflect on what has been causing poor communication. Please select as many options which fit your behavioral pattern from the list below.

- You often complain or are too busy picking at your partner's flaws.
- When things get difficult, you ignore them.
- You are too busy criticizing your partner that you cannot even hear them out.
- You are impatient and always get into fights.
- Expressing yourself to your partner is a rare phenomenon.

- You don't make an effort to talk to them.
- You act like it's all fine even when it is not.
- Whenever things go wrong, you always blame them.
- You fail to understand their problems.
- Hiding things is your specialty.
- You always assume the worst things about them.

Evaluating Your Triggers

- Are you agitated because your partner spends more than they save?
- Have you ever fought with your partner on the topic of kids?
- Are you getting angry recently due to the lack of attention your partner is giving you?
- Have you ever fought with them on the topic of in-laws?
- Is money always a cause of concern in your relationship?
- Are you irritated with your partner because they don't share the same goals as you (i.e., having kids, managing your finances, etc.)?

By answering these simple questions, you can identify the key triggers and learn to discuss them with your partner.

Chapter 3:

Step 3—The Magic Ingredients

Noah and Emma were at it again; the constant shouting and fighting without leaving any space for words to penetrate their minds. Emma was too busy with work at the office and accused Noah of not paying enough attention to her. However, Noah became too tired to defend himself all the time and make her understand his dilemma. He started shouting and accusing Emma of always wanting to complain rather than display any form of affection for all the hard work he does.

Both of them were too busy suffocating each other with words rather than listening to each other. Does this sound familiar to any of you? This is what most of us do when we are in a relationship, when we are too busy spewing words at our partners to listen to them express their frustrations. In the previous chapter, we began to discuss how listening can drastically improve your communication with your partner.

In this chapter, we will be going into the finer details, explaining the dynamics between hearing and listening in a relationship, how partners can learn to listen to each other, different ways partners can effectively influence each other by listening, different ways partners can validate their emotions, and lastly, we will reveal the magic ingredient to every happy relationship.

How Can Paying Attention Drastically Improve My Relationship?

Many partners constantly complain of their other half not listening to them or not paying enough attention to them. Have you ever experienced a phenomenon where you are too busy scrolling on social media while your partner is raising concerns about some problems in their life? Most of us are guilty of fiddling with our phones rather than paying attention to our partners. This seems like a minor issue, but it has been the major reason people fight a lot of the time. *He wasn't paying attention to what I just said. She is too busy uploading pictures on Instagram. He is more interested in watching that football match than having a conversation with me. She would rather play Minecraft than have a serious talk.*

These and more are some of the most prevalent statements you hear from people experiencing problems in their relationships. It just so happens that one partner loves being distracted while the other is busy making efforts to try to work things out. When things tilt to one side, they come crashing down, which happens at some point in most relationships. At some point, people get tired of complaining, but the recipients of complaints also experience some guilt. But before we dive into the details of how listening can improve your relationship, let us understand the basic difference between listening and hearing.

Listening vs Hearing: Are They the Same Thing?

If you went out on the street right now and asked someone the difference between listening and hearing, they would probably say it's the same thing. Before we give you the solution, it is important to understand the root cause of this problem. If your partner is complaining about their bad day and they suddenly notice you are distracted, they will point it out. At this point, you will probably tell them "*I can hear you, honey*" to reassure them, but were you really paying any attention?

So the basic difference between listening and hearing is that when you are hearing someone, you are in a passive mode, which means you can hear them talking, but you aren't focused on what they are saying. Either you are too busy thinking about something or doing something else which keeps you distracted. However, when you are listening to someone, you are in an active mode, paying attention to what they are saying, remembering all the small details so you can help them through it with reassurance and a solution, if requested.

What happens when someone is hearing rather than listening to you? They will never be able to comprehend what you are trying to say, let alone pay attention. All this time, you are trying to exclaim your frustrated feelings, but you will never get through their thick wall. This is exactly why people complain that their partners are not paying attention to them; because they are too busy hearing them complain and not listening to them express their emotions. Listening to your partner is also one form of respect you bestow upon them by letting them know that you can feel their emotions and understand that it must be difficult for them. If you have been too distracted by something and are unable to listen to your partner, it is time to change that. To help you develop an effective form of listening, let us discuss how you can empathize with your partner by listening to them.

How Do I Improve My Relationship by Listening Effectively?

Has it ever happened that you only hear certain accusations thrown at you while fighting with your partner and react to them? We all do this at some point. If your partner were to tell you today, "I have been dealing with this all alone and feeling vulnerable. It was pretty selfish of you to leave me alone." Here, the partner who is hearing will probably only pay attention to the last sentence where they were accused of being selfish rather than paying attention to what was said before. It is a human impulse, and many of us do this.

What would effective listening look like? Firstly, from the way your partner talks, you will understand that they are frustrated about something that has gone wrong. The next thing you need to do is endeavor to understand what went wrong, why they feel this way, etc. In the above example, the partner clearly states that they were dealing with something alone. In this case, you must listen to them and apologize this way: "I am so sorry you felt that way, it wasn't my intention." This will show your partner that you can empathize with what they went through, and they will feel grateful that you paid attention to the finer details.

Now, this isn't exactly an easy task. Your mind is predominantly occupied by this interesting tweet you read a few minutes ago. It is troublesome to pay attention to your partner when your monkey mind tells you to check out that tweet. So, how can you effectively listen to your partner when your mind is preoccupied with an article titled, "10 Ways to Make a Six-Figure Income Today?" In this section, we will discuss some techniques that can improve your listening skills and the health of your relationship.

- **Maintain eye contact**—One of my personal favorites and the quickest way to improve intimacy in your relationship is by maintaining eye contact with your partner. You must have heard this popular phrase, "Eyes are like windows to your soul." Your eyes can talk, they can reveal emotions and let your partner know how you feel. While talking to your partner, try to look into their eyes; you will be able to see their eyes sparkle when they are happy or their puffy eyes if they have been crying. Either way, eyes can reveal all the different emotions your partner feels when communicating.

- **Look at the body language**—Couples have a certain body language that they display while communicating with each other. For instance, partners in love with each other often face each other while talking to show their interest. On the contrary, anyone losing interest in their partner often shows evasive body language by facing away from them or avoiding eye contact. When your partner is facing some trouble, they will also display a certain body language that is anxious, irritated, or impatient. If you observe them closely, you will see how they end up misplacing things or getting annoyed while they shout on the phone. Body language is one way to ascertain your partner's emotions, and it is often hard to miss.

- **Nod your head in acknowledgement**—It may seem childish, but nodding your head is one way to let your partner know that you are listening to them without interrupting them. When you wish to acknowledge your partner while they are expressing themselves, you can nod your head and tell them, *I am listening to you, and I understand how you feel.* Your significant other will also feel encouraged by this gesture, and they will try to open up to you simply because you are a great listener.

- **Be understanding and show empathy**—When someone tries to talk about their difficult situation, we should always try to understand things from their perspective; think what they think and feel how they feel. Being empathetic is also an important trait when your partner communicates with you. Once your partner is done expressing themselves, you can always squeeze their hand and tell them, "I understand this is a difficult time for you." In this way, your partner knows that they have expressed themselves clearly, and they also feel relaxed when you show your understanding toward their feelings.

Additionally, while listening to your partner, avoid judging them, cutting them off, or, worse yet, shouting at them. When your partner tries to express themselves freely, they have the expectation that their significant other will listen to them, try to understand their feelings, and support them. Anything otherwise can throw them off and discourage them from approaching you the next time. By using all the above techniques, you are learning to listen effectively and encouraging your partner to express themselves in your company. We have already learned various techniques to listen effectively, but we will also touch upon different ways you can influence your partner to listen to you in the next section.

How Do I Get Them to Listen to Me?

Other than being a good listener, partners also have to learn the art of influencing their partners to listen to them. When I talk about influencing your partner, I mean how you approach your partner before communicating your feelings. Many people have this habit of beating around the bush, being negative, slinging verbal abuse, shouting, etc., which is off-putting. Nobody would want to listen to someone who is always trying to be rude while expressing themselves, including your partner. But there are ways through which you can influence them to listen to you, which are as follows.

Talk in a Calm Tone and Be Concise

When you approach your partner with some problem, you have to talk about it in a soothing tone. As a human being, feeling frustrated is valid, but if you start pointing fingers and blaming your partner, they will be upset, leading to an even bigger fight. Some of you may straight up get bossy with your partner and tell them, "Listen here! We need to talk, alright!" Doing this will make you feel more frustrated, your partner will get irritated, and the issues will remain at large without being solved. Instead, you can approach your partner and tell them, "Hey, can we talk? I want to talk about something that is bothering me." The tone is calm, collected, and concise, so your partner knows what you intend to do, and they know there will be no beating around the bush.

Stop Accusing and Take Ownership

We are all familiar with one of the biggest relationship problems out there; how easy it is to start pointing fingers when things go wrong. *You did this. It is all because of you.* At some point, your partner will be fed up with all the accusations and walk out the door. If you wish to talk about your grievances, we need to talk about ownership. When you take ownership, it encourages others to accept their errors and make amends as well. Taking ownership is the easiest way to encourage someone to listen to you. When all the blame shifts from 'you' to 'I,' partners start to realize where they went wrong and try to make amends. If you are in the wrong, always learn to say, "I am sorry. It was because of me." This way, you will not make your partner feel too guilty and upset while you discuss your issues.

Balance Out the Positives and Negatives

When things go wrong, we have all these negative thoughts telling us that it's over; there is no escape, as if our life has ended its course. That is never the case, since we like to exaggerate bad events in our minds all the time. Every emotion you feel is supported by an energy that will rub off on your partner. For example, if you are extra cheerful today, the people you surround yourself with will also feel those happy vibes. In the same way, your energy rubs off on your partner, so usually, when one partner is upset, the other person feels low, too. In such situations, you can learn to tackle the issue by balancing the positive and negative aspects of the situation. For instance, you can always express your support for your partner by telling them, "I love how you are always so understanding and supportive of me." This will make your partner feel better about the entire issue, and both of you can learn to have that little ray of hope while tackling the tough situation.

Other than this, you can always learn to pause the conversation. Think and reflect on your actions and words before you impulsively speak hurtful words. You must also ensure that you don't keep changing the subject and end up bringing something up from the past or fighting over a completely different issue irrelevant to your situation. The bottom line is that your partner will listen to you only if you learn to influence them in the right way.

Since you have learned different ways to listen effectively and influence your partner, in the next section, you will learn all about validation and why it matters in a relationship.

Validating Your Partner's Feelings

You must have come across some people who easily open up to you and talk about their problems occasionally. Have you ever thought about why these people always approach you? It's because they felt that you validated their feelings, and they felt that you would understand them. In any form of relationship, validation is very important. Validating someone is as good as letting them know that "I see you and I hear you." So many people feel trapped and misunderstood by others. If someone were to approach you and say, "My parents just divorced, and it has been taking a toll on me mentally. I feel so depressed all the time." Instead of validating their emotions, you say, "Yeah, well, it's all temporary. You'll get over it eventually. Just put a smile on and move on."

By doing this, you are not taking their feelings into account and just dumping your advice on them. *You'll get over it. It's all A-okay, don't worry. Why are you moping so much? It's not like that happened to you.* All these sentences are the simplest way to create problems in any relationship. It also shows the other person that you are not the least bothered by what went wrong in their life, and their presence is some form of annoyance you can't handle. However, the concept of emotional validation is the exact opposite of this because you show you are curious about the other person's feelings, and you go out of your way to reassure them. This small action from your end lets them feel that whatever they are going through—the emotions they feel, their thoughts, and the words they speak—are all understood and validated by you, making your bond stronger over time.

How Does Validation Work in a Relationship?

Validating your partner's feelings is one way to let them know that you can understand what they are going through, although you don't necessarily have to agree on their perspective. This is one form of respect you bestow upon your partner so that they realize that you are hearing them. No, validation isn't just something you do only during the most difficult times; you need to keep this in mind as often as you can.

For instance, your partner shares some exciting news about opening their new bakery. How do you validate their feelings in this case? Some partners are a bit unbothered by these things and show a lack of emotions, which translates to a lack of support, and your partner ends up feeling that *he didn't even look happy*. Instead, when you decide to validate your partner's feelings, you go, "Babe, I am so happy for you! It's so exciting that your dreams are finally becoming a reality." This way, your partner knows that their emotions are validated, and they can feel your support and encouragement through words and actions.

If we take the same example but for a difficult situation, say your partner had a stressful day at work. He comes home and sits on the couch with his head hanging low. When you approach them, they tell you all the horrible things that happened today and how it is bothering them. You can validate their feelings by squeezing their shoulders or hugging them and telling them, "Wow, you have had it rough lately. I am sure it is driving you crazy. I'd be frustrated, too, if I were you." When you say this, your partner will understand that their feelings have been validated. They will try to open up to you in small ways because they know you will always make the effort to relate to them.

When you combine the power of validation with effective listening, you are in for a treat. You will see how your relationship drastically improves when you adopt these techniques listed above, along with emotional validation. All these magic ingredients combine to improve your bond with your partner, heal your relationship, and make it healthier. But have you always wondered what secret ingredient could lead to happy relationships? It can't just be listening or communicating; there must be more, right? Well, let us take a look at the superpower that makes the most happy and successful relationships today.

The Secret Ingredient to a Happy Relationship

Every happy relationship is a combination of secret ingredients that lead to longevity. Couples fight and need some space to evaluate decisions in life, but that doesn't necessarily mean that your relationship is bad. Couples who are separated will say that marriage or a relationship will only make you unhappy. It isn't exactly their fault if their partner hurt them or they experienced some past relationship trauma. Relationships can get people down, and sometimes they hit rock bottom, but that doesn't mean you cannot overcome your difficulties and find happiness again. To help you understand how happy relationships last longer, we will list some of the factors that act as a superpower to lead to a successful connection and an everlasting bond.

Your Partner Is Your Priority

Any unhappy relationship has this one factor that partners always complain about, "I was never their/his/her priority." Prioritizing your partner doesn't mean sticking to them like glue 24 hours a day and letting them know how much you love them. That will make them think you're clingy, and it is off-putting. When we talk about relationship priority, it means you have to remove some time for your partner every day and talk to them. Spend some quality time with them by talking about your life, goals, work, and childhood memories, and let them know how much they matter to you. Every happy relationship sees an outcome where both people prioritize one another and realize how their presence matters in the other's life.

Commit Yourself to Your Partner

Every relationship should have trust and respect; without them, it will crumble. So many partners get cheated on, which makes it difficult for them to trust anyone in the future. When you commit yourself to your partner, you let them know that you will always be loyal to them for the rest of your life. Respect is yet another thing people underestimate in a relationship. Most separated couples involve partners complaining about how their ex-husband or ex-boyfriend never respected them, be it in terms of their choices, perspectives, or even their actions. If you do not respect your other half, the relationship will not last very long. Every successful relationship consists of two people who are completely loyal and respectful to each other.

Show Your Love Through Intimate Gestures

Love isn't just about saying the words "I love you" and calling it a day. Your partner knows more than anybody that you love them, especially when you say the words, but more than this, it is about showing them through your actions. Sneaking in a kiss on their forehead, hugging them after a tiring day, helping them with the chores, and being kind and affectionate to them are all the small gestures that make them understand that you love them. It has happened that partners who experience turbulence in their relationships often lack intimate gestures because they are keeping themselves at a distance and avoiding each other. But what happy couples do more than anyone is learn to forgive, and that is also one way to show your partner how much you love them. (We will be discussing forgiveness in relationships in Chapter 5.) Happy couples are the ones who are always showing their love for one another, keeping their relationship healthy and secure.

Focus on Positive Aspects

You will not like everything about your partner, be it their habits, behavior, or the way they act. Everyone in a relationship goes through this rough patch, and the only way to resolve this problem is by communicating with your partner. Beyond all the fights and the problems, we tend to focus on our partner's flaws, thinking *he is always running away while we talk. Why can't she take the trash out every day?* All these thoughts keep revolving around us, telling us how our partner is not good enough. However, a happy couple always tries to overlook their partner's flaws. This doesn't mean you overlook the toxic behavior but rather the small things that lead to unnecessary fights. Every successful relationship is a byproduct of the partners' positive attitudes which help them see the good points rather than only the flaws.

The other secret ingredients include how your family is supportive of this relationship; the way both of you face every problem; your unrelenting support for one another; the clear means of communication; and acknowledging your partner's feelings. All these factors lead to a happy and successful relationship. Most importantly, having a deeper understanding and willingness to compromise in a relationship is important. Lastly, love your partner for who they are rather than trying to make changes that will only lead to disappointment.

Since we have already discovered different ways to help relationships remain happy and successful, let us look next at how a couple gets stuck in an overly emotional state when they are fighting and the different ways to resolve this in the next chapter.

Key Takeaways

- Sometimes partners barely pay attention to what their significant other is saying, which causes problems in their relationship. Listening to your partner is one way to shower your attention upon them and make them feel like sharing their problems.

- When you validate your partner's feelings, you become one with them. It is your way of telling them that you are connected with everything they just said.

- The superpower for a happy and successful relationship involves paying careful attention to your partner by making them your priority, showing your love through intimate gestures, and committing yourself completely.

Application Workbook—3

Evaluating Focus

Distractions are everywhere, but our partners need us to focus on them when they express themselves. Through this exercise, we will put our focus to the test so that we can become aware of how much we pay attention. Select the choice which most applies to you from the choices below:

Your partner is sharing a horrible experience they had at the mall today. You are too busy

- Dreaming in your own world about that new game you played.
- Looking at them and observing their body language to understand how they feel.

When your partner is discussing something serious, you always

- Pay attention to them to understand what went wrong.
- Keep yourself distracted about a Super Bowl match.

Your partner is sharing their work promotion with you and they seem happy. This achievement also

- Is very exciting, and you congratulate your partner on their career progress.
- Boring. Progress is how we move. You are more interested in watching a new movie tonight.

Your partner is very upset about something and they are trying to share this with you. You ensure that

- You make eye contact and squeeze their hands, encouraging them to talk.
- You keep thinking *here we go again!* while you remain distracted.

If the majority of your answers tilt toward supporting your partner and paying attention to them, you know you are effectively listening to them. Based on the test, if you are distracted and not considering your partner's feelings, you now know that you are making them feel uncomfortable, leaving you both in an awkward position.

Journaling on Your Relationship Superpower

Note down some things in the workbook that inform you about the superpower of your relationship. It can be along the lines of

- We always understand each other.
- When I am going through difficulty, he/she is always there to support me.
- He/she always listens to me and helps me resolve my issues.
- I am always their number-one priority.
- Even when he/she is agitated, they always express themselves calmly.
- He/she values and respects me in this relationship.
- If I am upset, he/she does their best to leave a smile on my face.
- During every meaningful conversation, he/she opens up to me.
- If he/she makes a mistake, they always apologize first without being prideful.
- He/she always brings out the best in me and helps me see the bright side.

You can make additions along these lines or even write some other things regarding the superpower in your relationship. Whenever you are going through a difficult time in your relationship, you can always go back and read what you wrote. Every relationship has the superpower to overcome difficult times. By journaling and reflecting, you are reminding yourself about the secret ingredients your relationship holds.

Chapter 4:

Step 4–Stuck in the Mud

Noah was busy doing some plumbing work, since the taps in the kitchen were continuously leaking and they needed repair. While he was busy fixing this problem, Emma suddenly called out his name. He turned his back and saw that she had some papers in her hand. Frowning, Noah asked Emma, "What is it? Can't you see I am busy fixing this tap?" Emma was already angry about something, and hearing those words wasn't exactly what she needed. "I don't care what it is that you are doing. What is the meaning of this? You forgot to pay the bills again this month. It was your responsibility, Noah! I asked you to take care of one thing, and this is what you do."

Before this incident, Noah had a short argument with his boss regarding one of their clients, which got him in a sour mood. To distract his brain from this incident, he decided to fix the tap. Unaware of Noah's circumstances, Emma was bashing him with her complaints, indirectly telling him that he couldn't handle his responsibilities. Noah suddenly started shouting, "Emma, I don't understand. What is your problem? Can't you see I am fixing this already? I am well aware of my responsibilities. Stop taking a dig at me, for God's sake." Noah knew he was wrong, but the way Emma spoke to him threw him off. He just decided to ignore Emma while she was triggered. She was ready to spew all the ugly things that came to her mind.

From the above instance, one thing is clear: both the partners are emotionally overwhelmed. We all have triggers that can get us angry or depressed as human beings. Chapter 2 laid down many relationship triggers that can lead to fights between couples. We also have particular individual emotional triggers that can cause us to become upset. When we are overly emotional, we fail to communicate with our partners, which can cause misunderstandings. To help you avoid being in such a state and openly communicate with your partner, we will list different ways to overcome your emotions and offer techniques to help you calm down when you are triggered, giving you the power to press the pause button.

Emotional State: How Does This Affect My Relationship?

Every relationship has its testing times when couples lose their minds and start arguing. *She is driving me crazy with all the small things. He is never doing anything the right way.* These complaints are an outcome of the small triggers that set people off. Usually, when we are triggered about some sensitive topic, our first reaction is to take a verbal swing at our partner by thinking, *Oh, you think you are better at this? Let me show you.* Especially if your pride is hurt, you may want to tell your partner that they are in the wrong aggressively.

What happens when a partner is experiencing an emotional state? The first thing that the typical couple does is obstruct their communication. This can be in any form; you might either start fighting by throwing ugly comments at each other, or you completely shut your partner out and let them fend for themselves. In this way, you are not addressing any issues, which means the problem still exists while both become exhausted and feel overly emotional. The second thing that happens is that when a couple is stuck in an overly emotional state, they lack any understanding and have zero insight into what went wrong. It's like this; an angry bull only wants to knock off anyone coming in his way without seeing why the person was there in the first place. The overly emotional state is like a blindfold that prevents us from seeing the logical side of any given circumstance.

When either of the partners is emotionally affected by something, they will never think rationally. This means that when you are angry with your partner, you tell them all the bad things you have otherwise stored deep within your heart. None of these things you tell them are true, but it all comes out and hurts them because you are triggered at that moment. We are human beings bound to feel this way, but there are ways to control your emotional state without hurting your relationship. If you have been suffering from an overly emotional state, especially in your relationships, this next section will help you overcome this using specific techniques.

How Do I Overcome My Emotional State?

Every relationship thrives on emotions, which help you relate to each other and understand one another. The emotion of love helps you get together with your significant other and stay with them till the end. But there is a dark side to these emotions, which we discussed above. You might feel overly emotional at times, whatever the reason. It could be due to personal loss, loneliness, a feeling of detachment, your partner not prioritizing you, etc. Have you ever observed that your emotions sway you from seeing when your partner is making efforts to support you? We saw one of these examples in Chapter 2 where Emma lost her father and became overstimulated by her grief. She couldn't open up to Noah, and this affected their relationship. So the question is, what can you do to overcome your emotional state? The following techniques will help you control your emotions better in the face of difficult situations, enabling you to communicate with your partner.

Use "I" Instead of Saying "You"

How is saying "I" even related to overcoming your emotional state? Well, it does have a connection. Remember that one time you got so upset and told your partner, "You always do as you please!" The major problem is that it is an indirect way of complaining and nitpicking when you keep saying "you." The same sentence is like screaming in your partner's face, saying that *you are the problem here*. As a result, your partner gets agitated and the fight begins. How about you start using this instead: "I feel very upset when you don't take my feelings into consideration." It is a simple sentence, but it will help your partner realize what you feel instead of hearing you complain. Through this method, they can consider your feelings more carefully without feeling bad about themself.

Take Some Time Off

When you are angry with your partner, your blood is pumping and all you want to do is fight with them to let them know how this affects you. We do this from time to time when we are angry. However, this isn't exactly healthy behavior. If you keep doing this every time you are angry, your partner will get tired eventually and think that they are better off without you. In this situation, you can try using the technique of taking some time off and being by yourself. You don't have to separate from your partner; rather, take some time and space to evaluate your emotions before getting agitated and starting another fight. Once you have figured out what is upsetting you, you can lay all your cards before your partner and have a mature conversation rather than screaming at the top of your lungs.

On the other hand, if you feel that you are getting agitated over an argument, you can tell your partner, "I am sorry, but I would like some time away before we discuss this issue." By doing so, you are making your partner aware that you aren't walking away from the problem but rather taking some space to collect your thoughts and emotions before speaking again. We will discuss this in a much more detailed manner when we talk about the power of the 'pause' button in the latter half of the chapter.

Don't Point at Their Shortcomings

When we are angry with our partners, we like to dig their graves and make them see all the mistakes they have made in their life, even though last time they made this mistake, you said, "It's okay. I understand this can happen from time to time." Yet here you are, bringing up the same issue. This is one of the cheapest tricks in the book to guilt trip someone. Even if you argue about not taking the dog for a walk or forgetting to pay the bills, never bring up another issue at hand, like how they bailed on your date last night. It will make your partner feel very guilty and upset. Just focus on the issue at hand and do your best to resolve things in the present so that you can spend some quality time with your partner.

Look on the Bright Side

What makes an already problematic situation even more depressing is that we have all these negative thoughts. Sometimes they are self-degrading thoughts telling you that you are not good enough. *What does he even see in me? What am I even doing here?* Sometimes it can be negative thoughts related to a situation, like, *What if they leave me? What if she is cheating on me?* Without clarity on the given situation, having such thoughts makes it harder for you to cope. In such cases, you need to overcome these negative emotions by having positive thoughts. Think of all the times your partner supported you, cherished you, and expressed their gratitude toward you. You can think of all the bright moments you spent with your partner so that you don't feel low about a temporary situation. Through this technique, you might learn to relax and take a break from the overthinking syndrome.

All these techniques will help you overcome your emotional state in the best way possible without needing to argue with your partner unnecessarily. Of course, these are not the only things you can do. These are simply different ways to avoid getting into a tiff with your partner. Controlling your emotional state by yourself requires some practice and a different approach. To help you calm down from an overly emotional state at an individual level, there are various methods listed here that can help you and enable you to evaluate these emotions and share them with your partner.

Different Ways You Can Calm Yourself in an Emotional State

We learned previously that various approaches can help you control your emotions when you are having a difficult time with your partner. Most of the time, our emotions are most stimulated when we are alone.

For example, consider the feeling of anxiety; it is typically brought on by the overwhelming thoughts you have when you are alone. So even if we learn to stabilize our emotions while having a conversation, it doesn't necessarily negate the fact that at some point, we will feel insecure or worried about something when we are alone. To help you overcome this, we will be listing some of the most basic techniques you can follow to calm yourself when you are overstimulated. If you feel anxious or depressed due to a certain situation, these approaches will help you figure out your feelings and tackle the situation in front of you.

Take a Deep Breath

Something which is often labeled overrated these days is the feeling of taking a break from your overburdened schedule and just trying to breathe. When you feel anxious due to any difficult situation, the first things that happen are the eerie feeling in the pit of your stomach, your heart beating fast due to worry or fear, and your head feeling heavy from all these thoughts in your mind. The best solution to this problem is to take a seat and then inhale a deep breath. Hold it for a second and then exhale. Try doing this at least 4-5 times, and you will feel a bit refreshed. All that tension in your body and the worries in your brain will disappear momentarily. You will feel a lot calmer, and you will have clear thoughts about your current problem.

Maintain a Thought Journal

What people underestimate most of the time is writing their thoughts down. Who wants to make that effort, right? It's just thoughts that will flow like wind and disappear like a dandelion. However, at times, you will not be able to let things go. *Why is this happening to me? Why am I feeling this way?* Overthinking is another way of putting yourself in an overwhelming soup that stimulates your emotions. If you want to calm yourself in such a situation, you can always journal your thoughts. Journaling is a historical method that has been used from the time of Marcus Aurelius, the former Roman emperor, to help people collect their thoughts. You can always start by noting down how you are feeling. Next, evaluate these and categorize, such as:

- Why am I feeling this way?
- What caused me to feel this way? Was it a person or a situation?
- If you start to feel better, you can always note that down, too.
- What can I learn from this situation?
- How do I overcome this if I feel it again?

By maintaining a journal, you are talking to yourself, which can help you discover many things about yourself and also help you clear your head.

Go for a Warm Bath

Bathrooms are indeed the best place to get creative and have imaginative thoughts. But that is not the point here; the point is that taking a warm bath in your tub can be relaxing for the body and the mind. Most people can think clearly in a bathroom because when our mind is relaxed, we can think of different ways to tackle any situation or get creative. Most of us think of solutions to our problems when we are in a bathroom or busy showering! Taking a warm bath will divert your mind from its anxious state, which will help you to cool down and take a breather.

Meditate for a Minute

Meditation can be a difficult technique, especially if you are a mind-wanderer exploring different scenarios with your eyes closed. But let us try something new today. Close your eyes for exactly one minute and breathe. During this period, ensure that you do not think of anything. Just practice mindful meditation and relax for a minute there. As a beginner to meditation practice, this can be a great start. You can slowly increase it to two minutes or even five minutes a day. The reason I asked you to meditate for one minute is because most of us are busy with a packed schedule and always excuse ourselves from doing anything relaxing. Even if you meditate for a minute with a busy schedule, it will be like a short break that will lighten the burden and ease your emotions.

Beyond all these small techniques, also consider exercise, like going on a morning jog or an evening walk to refresh yourself. You can listen to some light music while cooking or cleaning the house and at the same time enjoy the process. Lastly, the key to remaining calm is to focus on the task at hand. If you walk with your dog, focus your attention on them instead of thinking about your boss blowing up in a meeting. When we cut down on all the unnecessary things in our lives, it becomes easier to remain calm and collected.

There is one last superpower that can help you remain calm and in control of your emotions in any given situation: the power of the pause button. We will be discussing this concept in much greater detail in the next section.

The Power of a Pause Button

The power of the pause button is a well-known concept in business communications. Great leaders always pause momentarily to think before they speak their minds. Pause is an essential concept in any form of communication. When someone hurts us, we want to give it back to them. With the pause button in your hand, you press it momentarily and think, *Does it hurt? Yes, it does. Is there a need to make a big scene here? Not really.* So what you do instead is brush this off by saying, "I understand that you may not have much choice in the matter, so you chose this path; however, was it necessary?" This way, you can still have a proper conversation and remain composed. Let us see how we can use this concept in terms of relationships.

How to Harness the Power of the Pause Button

In relationships, the power of pause comes in handy. When we want to go to our partner and start shouting, like Noah and Emma were doing in the introduction, we can just hit the pause button and avoid this uproar. For instance, in the introduction, we see how Noah tells Emma that she should be grateful since he works hard and earns money to provide her with the best life. In any given situation, it is valid for Emma to lose her cool, but instead of fighting with Noah, she hits the pause button here.

Emma takes a deep breath, and after collecting her thoughts, she says, "Sweetheart, I know you are working hard. I can understand your frustration, and we have not been spending enough time together. It is a bit upsetting because I want to spend some quality time with you and have a decent conversation." After hearing this, Noah is taken aback, and he instantly cools down. Using the pause button, Emma helps herself by remaining calm and having a clean conversation with him, allowing him to cool down and see things clearly.

Sometimes in a really difficult situation where both parties cannot control their emotional state, the power of the pause button acts as a peacemaker. Going back to the same example, Emma and Noah keep fighting. Both cannot come to an understanding here. Instead of resolving this issue, it is becoming bigger and consuming their energy. Noah finally has enough of it and hits the pause button. "Hey Emma, I understand you are frustrated, but can we take a break here? I can't seem to think straight at the moment. Let us talk about this after some time, shall we?" This way, Noah and Emma both go to their own respective spaces and evaluate their emotions so they can finally have a productive conversation. The pause button may seem easy to use, but it isn't easy all the time. To help you use it effectively, let us discuss how the pause agreement works between partners.

The Pause Agreement: Hold It Right There, We Need to Pause!

The power of the pause button is a simple yet effective strategy that can help you improve your relationship and communicate with ease. There are many different ways you can use the pause button in a relationship. The most basic way to tell your partner that you need to take a pause is this: whenever you get the itching impulse to say something that could potentially hurt your partner, or if you need to cool down for a minute, you can always use phrases like:

- Sorry, I may need some time to cool off.
- I am getting a bit agitated right now. Let's stop, please.
- I can't think clearly. Can we take a break?
- This is so triggering and I need a timeout.

These are some phrases that you can use when you feel that you might blow up or you cannot communicate clearly. There will be times when you cannot say that you need a pause, maybe because you are anxious to resolve this soon or you are very frustrated with your partner. In this case, you can establish something known as "pause signals" with your partner, like small keywords such as 'timeout,' 'pause,' or 'stop.' This way, your partner understands that you need some space and time to think clearly before conversing with them.

The aftermath of the pause signal is also something that you must consider. Sometimes one partner may take longer than the other to recover. This is why both partners should have a conversation only after both have calmed down. If you are going to be agitated while you talk, it will only lead to another fight, which means you are moving in circles with no clear outcome. Even if you have calmed down, wait till your partner has also collected their thoughts, and then you can easily address all the problems. Also, while trying to bury the hatchet, always start by saying, "I am sorry if I hurt you. I was out of line." Apologizing makes it all worth having the conversation. You can also tell your partner that it'll be okay as you both face this together.

The power of pause works wonders when you implement it in your relationship. With the help of all these techniques, be it those that calm you down or help you take some time away like the pause button, you can manage your emotions better and learn to communicate healthily. But if there is anything that we have learned through this journey, it is that either partner can become agitated and say something mean or even aggressive with their words. We sometimes grudge against our partners because we cannot forgive them. However, forgiveness is the most crucial element in any relationship. To help you understand this, we will discuss how partners can seek forgiveness and how they can learn to accept, forgive, and let go to heal their relationship.

Key Takeaways

- An overly emotional state is overwhelming for every partner, causing unnecessary fights in your relationship. You can overcome this by simply taking some time off, talking about problems in the context of 'I' rather than 'you,' and thinking about the positive aspects of your relationship.

- When you feel anxious, relax yourself by doing some activity, like writing down your thoughts, meditating for a minute, etc., to get a grip on your thoughts and stabilize your emotions.

- The power of the pause button is an effective technique that helps you take some time off whenever you feel agitated about something. This way, you are bound to resolve things faster without having any arguments.

Application Workbook—4

Assessing Emotional Triggers

Go through this list of sentences to help you identify what gets you emotionally triggered. Once you have found your answers, you can talk to your partner about this, explaining what really riles you up and how you can fix it.

Pick up your workbook and note this down: **I get emotionally triggered when...**

1.
2.
3.

You can note down any thing and as many as apply. For example, you can use the above technique this way: I get emotionally triggered when...

1. My partner starts complaining about something without considering the right time and situation.
2. They never appreciate what I do for them.
3. I have had a difficult day but my partner doesn't pay attention to me.

You can also note down anything that was triggered due to some incident or the people surrounding you and how that emotionally triggered you. Once you note that down, you can talk to your partner about this, as you now have clarity on what led to your emotional state.

The Pause Agreement

Through this pause agreement, you can establish some predefined terms that will allow you to cool down whenever you are in the middle of an argument or having a heated discussion.

Give a pause signal to your partner when...

- You feel frustrated during a discussion and believe that you will emotionally react.
- You are triggered by your partner's behavior and need to assess the situation.
- You want to impulsively react by telling them off.
- You are not getting a grip on the situation and need some space.
- You are really annoyed with your partner and need some time.
- You haven't figured out why you are emotionally overwhelmed.
- You need some time to recollect your thoughts.
- You want to fight with them over certain issues.

If you feel any of the above emotions, you must take a pause. Always give a signal to your partner, saying, "I need some space," or simply use the secret pause signal that has been mutually decided upon by both of you.

Chapter 5:

Step 5–Remove All Obstacles

Emma and Noah were at it again, and the ugly fight resulted in a heated exchange of hurtful words. Emma shouts, "Noah, why are you always this selfish? I have been keeping my cool, but did you have to act like that in front of our friends?" Noah stands in front of Emma and repeats, "Emma, I don't care what your friends think. You know Richard was taking a dig at me. Why do you always have to take their side?" Richard was one of Emma's friends and someone who would speak without a second thought. He was taking a swing at Noah by insulting his profession subtly, which got him enraged. Although Richard was wrong here, this led to a tiff between the loving couple.

Emma realized that Noah was triggered by what had happened at the hangout and said the words "time out." Since she uttered the pause signal, Noah didn't say anything. Both partners retreated into their own space and thought over the whole issue. After two hours, Noah came out of the room and approached Emma, sitting on the couch in the living room. "Hey Em, can we talk? I am sorry about my behavior before. I shouldn't have done that even though Richard started it." Emma looked over at Noah and signaled for him to sit beside her. "Noah, I know Richard was in the wrong, and I am sorry for arguing with you. You know how he is, and we shouldn't let such people get to us. I love you and respect you for what you do. It's okay, but please ignore him next time." After this, the loving couple forgave their errs and hugged each other.

Forgiveness forms the most important aspect of any relationship. It is the most difficult aspect, too, if you ask me. Many couples who have been in love for many years separate after many years of togetherness because they fail to overlook the flaws and forgive their significant other. Forgiveness is one form of freedom for an individual. When you forgive, you accept that the person has committed a mistake and then let it go. By doing so, you are releasing yourself from all the stress and the heavy load of holding a grudge so you can live your life.

In a relationship, when a partner holds a grudge against their other half's actions, they will keep finding flaws and fighting with them over and over again. Over time, this weighs heavily on the couple, and they eventually go their separate ways. That is why in this chapter, we will discuss the importance of forgiveness, why partners should forgive each other, the process of softening your heart, and how talking to each other matters.

Importance of Forgiveness in a Relationship

Before we talk about the significance of forgiveness, let us discuss why we forgive in the first place. Why do people who have been through the most horrible experiences of their life learn to forgive others? It is because forgiveness is also a form of healing. When you have a grudge against something, the first thing that you do is hold onto it. What happens when you hold onto a knife? It keeps cutting you, and you keep bleeding. In other words, you are always in pain. Having a grudge against something means you are holding onto that pain and suffering, preventing you from moving on in life. Forgiving is essentially letting go of the pain and suffering and giving yourself the freedom to experience life again. Now, how does this work in a relationship?

Your partner happens to say something terrible which hurts you, or they do something terrible, like lying to you, which hurts your trust, and you develop this small grudge against them. *Why did he lie to me? Shouldn't he be sharing his life moments with me?* Sometimes we are so hurt by our partner's actions that we remember them for months or even years and bring them up during a much later fight. We take a dig at their pride and let them know how they did us wrong a long time ago. It can be quite a shock for your other half, and usually, they will be taken aback by this behavior. Have you ever heard your partner say,

"Why are you bringing it up after all this time? I thought we were past that."

This leads to yet another fight, and you are thrown back into the never-ending cycle of arguments that weigh down heavily on your mind, body, and soul. But with forgiveness, you can escape this trap and let it all go. Your partner lies to you but apologizes for that, so you forgive them. If your partner says hurtful words and comes back to say, "I am sorry for saying those things, I didn't mean them," then let them go. Stop holding onto those painful experiences that disturb not only your mind but also create disruptions in your relationship. If your partner's words or actions hurt you, you can always have an open conversation regarding this and overcome it together.

How Do I Cultivate the Willingness to Forgive?

Forgiving can be a painful process because even when we want to let it go, we can't help but hold onto it, right? After fighting with your partner for a long time, you may start developing a certain level of resentment toward them. Each time you fight, that resentment will grow. When you finally let that anger wash away and forgive your partner, you will create a stronger bond with your partner. See, every relationship has to grow at some point because if you don't, your relationship remains stagnant.

Although resentment can create a rift between a couple, the willingness to forgive will provide the right amount of healing and growth in the relationship. It is always our choice whether we wish to hold on to something or let it go. In that sense, forgiving our partner is also a choice. When we learn to forgive them, we learn to live in harmony with our other half and love them unconditionally. However, the road to forgiveness isn't an easy one. To help you in this journey, we will list various techniques that you can use to navigate your way through the entire process.

Learn to Apologize and Express Your Feelings

The first step to forgiveness is apologizing to your partner and communicating with them. Some partners like to do things without discussing them with their other half because they believe their partner will look down on their decisions. That is why many of us hide and do things until our partner finds out, and it all leads back to a household war. If you ever do something without consulting your partner, always approach them softly and apologize. "I am sorry I didn't tell you. I thought you wouldn't like it." This will help them understand why you did it and also help them forgive you.

On the other hand, if you don't like your partner doing something behind your back, talk about this with them. You can always say, "Sorry, but I did not like you buying that car without discussing it with me. We're supposed to be a team, you know." It makes your partner realize that they are wrong and they will usually apologize for their mistake. This is one way to avoid big fights and learn to forgive your partner easily.

Apologize Like You Mean It

'Sorry' is the most common word used today. You can do something wrong and say sorry to get over it without considering someone else's feelings. Sorry isn't just a simple word, it is a heartfelt apology, like saying something like, *I know I am wrong, and I will not do this again*. What is the point of apologizing to someone if you are bound to repeat your mistakes? It is common in a relationship to throw hurtful words toward your partner and say sorry. "I am sorry, I shouldn't have said it," you say, but after a week, you are fighting again and saying the same things. So, the second thing you need to learn in a relationship is to apologize meaningfully and ensure that you don't repeat the same mistakes. Don't say those hurtful words again if you are sorry. Avoid sneaking behind your partner's back to purchase something when you know they don't like it. By doing this, you are making your apology worth something and showing your partner that their forgiveness was meaningful and your relationship is getting stronger.

Forgive From the Bottom of Your Heart

"I forgive you" aren't just plain words that you can say and still hold a grudge against your partner. Truly forgiving someone means letting go of any form of resentment you hold toward them. The last step to forgiving someone is to forgive them from the bottom of your heart. So many partners bare their entire soul in front of their other half in the most vulnerable state. If, in this case, you were to still hold a grudge after saying that you forgive them, it would simply hurt them. "I thought you said you forgive me?" is what they will probably say later. So if you are going to forgive someone, forgive them from the bottom of your heart; otherwise, you can always let them make it up to you before forgiving them. There is no point in lying to your partner, who will only get hurt in the future during your fights.

These three are the most basic steps you can use, along with validation and the power of pause, to help you through the journey of forgiveness. By holding a grudge, we stand against our beloved, weakening our will to fight. With a willingness to forgive, you will unite with your partner and overcome any difficult situation together. However, there is one thing you must keep in mind; forgiveness exists for those who wish to learn from their mistakes and improve. Toxic relationships often don't have the strength to overcome, so forgiving your toxic partner only brings you more suffering. Willingness to forgive should be cultivated in your relationship to make it healthy and peaceful. In the next section, we will learn about softening of the heart and how forgiveness can help you with this process.

How Does Forgiveness Help With Softening the Heart?

Softening your heart holds significant value in relationships. Many people have a hard time softening their hearts. This may be an outcome of their traumatic past, as discussed in Chapter 1. Many people consider softening up to their partner to be a weakness. Why should you be the weak one in the relationship anyway? However, this is a misconception, and a classic one. Softening your heart means forming an affectionate bond with your partner and caring for them. You do your best to develop a safe bond with them so they feel they can open up to you wholeheartedly. Remember that first time you fell in love with your partner and felt that warm fuzzy feeling in your heart? When you love someone, you want to protect them and shower them with all the care and affection in this world. These feelings that you have felt for a long time are part of the process of softening your heart.

In the introduction, we highlighted how Noah and Emma slowly moved away from their honeymoon phase and started fighting with each other. Both of them exchanged harsh words, and suddenly the warmth from their relationship disappeared. Many of us have lost this warm and caring bond with our partners. It is an outcome of constant clashes and grudges. This is where the process of softening the heart comes into the picture. You have to learn to cultivate the same feeling of warmth you felt toward them when you fell in love. How do we do this? The most simple way is to communicate with them: What went wrong? Why is this happening to us? How can we resolve this? After you have figured out your problem, find a solution. For instance, if one of the partners is wrong, they should apologize, and the other should learn to forgive.

Forgiveness is the best way to soften your heart. When you care for your partner, you do your best to understand them and the situation. If your partner were to lie about something, even though lying is wrong, a small apology should soften your heart and let you forgive them. The misunderstanding starts and grows when we fail to understand why our partner did something. *Did my partner lie because they were ashamed to tell me?* Think about it from a different perspective, and you will see it. We need to seek a deeper understanding of our partner in a relationship to enable us to soften our hearts toward them. Since we have touched upon the topics of forgiveness and softening the heart, let us also take a look at why the way you talk to your partner matters in a relationship.

The Way We Talk to Each Other

Chapter 2 briefly touched upon how communication breakdown results from couples fighting with one another on issues without paying attention to how they speak. One of the partners forgets to pay the bills, and the other is too busy reprimanding them for neglecting their responsibility. We saw these instances before when we spoke about Noah and Emma fighting over forgetting to take out the trash or walk the dog. Even when your patience is running thin, you must learn to speak respectfully with your partner. They are human beings, and at some point, we all are bound to forget a thing or two and make mistakes. This doesn't mean that you should start pointing fingers and blaming them in a rude tone. The way you talk to your partner is very important, especially the tone and the words you use during the conversation. Here are some of the reasons why the way you talk to your significant other matters.

Disrespectful Tone Leads to Agitation

While fighting with your partner, using a disrespectful or sarcastic tone is a big no-no. When we are frustrated about something, we tend to say things disrespectfully, taking a dig at our partner or mocking them to let them know they are wrong. Both these approaches lead to more fights, and couples get tired in the end. If you continue to disrespect your partner verbally, they might have difficulty letting it go, and some partners may even tilt toward separation. Respect is of utmost importance in a relationship. No matter how agitated you are, talking about something in a respectfully calm tone is important. Lay the cards on the table in a respectful way, and your partner may want to communicate further and resolve the problems rather than run away from you.

Frequent Complaining Is Emotionally Overwhelming

Some partners are constantly complaining about everything going wrong in their lives. They are a bit pessimistic about life and even complain when you try something new. Complaining is also associated with negative energy, which overwhelms a person easily. It can get discouraging, especially if you fail to pay attention to the subject you wish to address. Suppose you have issues with your partner skipping their chores or forgetting their responsibilities. In that case, you can always openly converse about it, but don't forget to appreciate them for all their hard work. For instance, you complain to your partner, "You didn't take the trash out again. Why can't you do one thing properly?" This is bound to overwhelm your partner when you keep complaining about things, especially minor things like trash. Instead, you can always say this: "Hey, there was something I wanted to tell you. I appreciate how hard you work every day for our family. Would it be okay for you to take the trash out for the next week since you weren't able to do it for quite some time?" When you talk this way, you essentially appreciate them for everything they have done for you and give them a slight nudge about their responsibilities. Your partner will feel grateful that instead of complaining, you just went ahead and requested for them to do something. A polite request is less likely to be declined.

Speaking Without a Second Thought Is Destructive

When we are irked about something, we get impulsive and may confront our partners in a shallow way. Getting triggered about something makes us so anxious that we open our mouths without a second thought. For example, one partner is utterly disgusted by how their partner canceled date night and went out with their colleagues. Being annoyed by this situation, they quickly blurted out, "I hope you had a great time being surrounded by the people who don't even care about you." This comment enraged their other half, and the fight began. Sometimes our partner will do certain things that upset us, but there is a way to properly convey your emotions. What if the partner just took a moment by themselves and then said, "I didn't like the idea of you canceling our date night just to go out with your colleagues." This is a simple sentence that helps you convey your feelings in a calm tone without saying any gibberish that will upset your partner.

From all the above factors, we have understood one thing: the way we talk to our partners also determines the health of our relationship.

Suddenly disrespecting your partner, throwing back swear words, or mocking them isn't exactly an ideal way to have a conversation in the first place. When we go beyond all these things and pay careful attention to these minor factors, we can learn to communicate well with our partners.

With the help of this chapter, I hope you can learn the art of forgiveness and heal your relationship with your soulmate. Since we have already spoken about forgiveness, let us talk about trust. In the next chapter, we will be discussing how couples can build trust in their relationship and develop a safe environment while checking in on each other.

Key Takeaways

- Forgiveness helps you let go of the most painful experiences of your life and gives you the freedom to enjoy being in a healthy relationship. The willingness to forgive your partner helps you heal your relationship and grow together.

- Softening of the heart enables you to cultivate care and warmth in your relationship. By being soft toward your partner, you learn to forgive them quickly because they matter to you.

- The way you speak with your partner matters because partners are sensitive about disrespectful tones used against them. The way you talk to your partner shows how much you respect and understand them, which is another factor that leads to a successful relationship.

Application Workbook—5

Exercise Forgiveness

Sometimes our partners do things which can hurt us. It can take some time for you to forgive them. Through this exercise, you are going to first note down the situations where your partner was wrong, and later you will assess the situation and figure out ways to forgive them.

I am angry with my partner because…

1.
2.
3.

You can note down any reason here, be it your partner lying to you about something or taking action on something even when you both agreed against it. Whatever it is, just write it down here like this: "I am angry with my partner because they lied to me about their dinner plans."

So here, I have noted down my problem, now we will assess the situation. Why did your partner lie to you? Was it because something came up? You both must have had a fight and discussed why this situation took place. In the next section here, note down your *why*.

Why did my partner lie to me? "An urgent project came up and they were embarrassed to say no, so they lied about it."

After this, you must contemplate and understand the situation from their perspective. Remain cool and calm and try talking to them. Forgiveness isn't easy, but at some point you will learn to eventually let it go. You can note this down as well:

I was finally able to forgive and let it go because...
1. My partner sincerely gave a heartfelt apology.
2. They accepted that they were wrong.
3. They promised to never do this again.

By using these techniques, you will be able to assess the situation and take the first step toward forgiveness.

Chapter 6:

Step 6–Develop an Iron Trust

Emma and Noah were going through a rough patch in their relationship. A few days ago, they argued about Noah's new consulting venture, which he started a while back. With a new startup, it was hard for him to spend time with her, and he often bailed on dates. Emma had been upset about this, but she never brought it up. One day she went to him and said, "Hey babe, my parents have called us over for a family dinner on Tuesday. Could you please come with me, pretty please?" Noah knew he had been stuck with work lately, so he decided to go. "Yes, Em, I'll come with you. I am sorry for not being able to go out all this while. I promise we'll go to the family dinner on Tuesday."

Tuesday slowly arrives, and Noah is jammed with big investors' meetings, forgetting his dinner plans with Emma. Around late evening, he calls Emma and tells her, "Hey Em, sorry, I am a bit stuck here. There were tons of meetings today. I might get home a little late." Emma starts shouting from the other side, "Noah, you promised that we would have dinner with our parents. You're again bailing on me. I just can't take this," and she hangs up. For a second, Noah was deep in thought until it struck him that he completely forgot about the family dinner. He broke the promise he made to Emma.

Emma felt broken. Her partner had been bailing on her for a while now. She was afraid that he might be losing interest. This is usually the beginning stage of trust issues where your partner feels insecure or has a feeling that they will be abandoned. Emma developed trust issues after Noah broke too many promises and bailed on her every time they planned a date. Noah arrives home and realizes that Emma will surely be upset with this. *How should I make it up to her? How can I get my partner to trust me again?* To help you answer these questions, in this chapter, we will be discussing various ways you can cultivate trust in your relationship, develop a safe environment for your partner, and check in with them to overcome these issues.

How Do I Develop a Safe Environment for My Partner?

Trust issues are a common concern that every couple faces in a relationship. Most basic forms of trust issues result from lies or broken promises, where one partner is all words and no action. When someone promises you candy but never shows up, it is bound to be frustrating and will make you think, *That person was lying. Let's not trust them.* In a relationship, too, partners make high-end promises, like buying that big house. "That expensive car will be ours." "Let's grace our extravagant date night by going to a 5-star restaurant." All of these seem dreamy, but your partner fails to get any of them when the time comes. *I thought he said we'd buy a big house, yet we are cramped in this small space.* Sometimes we tell small lies at the beginning of a relationship because we are afraid they might leave if we have nothing to offer.

Other times, people lie when they don't wish to open up about their life. Over time, this will create trust issues when their partner has zero clue on what has happened in their life. When two people fall in love, they do their best to open up and talk about what they love, how they struggled, etc., so that their other half knows every little thing about them. So, if one day you come to know that your partner conveniently left out a series of things that happened in their life, it is bound to violate your trust. There is a way to overcome these trust issues. Partners won't typically lie to you purposefully unless you are in a toxic relationship with a pathological liar. Some of us lie out of fear, embarrassment, and guilt because we don't want our significant half to see us in a certain light. Either way, this road does lead to trust issues between a couple, so how do you resolve it?

Three Ways You Can Rebuild Trust In Your Relationship

Trust is the foundation of any relationship. It drives each partner to act loyally toward the other while putting their complete faith in them. We trust our partners over time because we know that they would never hurt us in any way and will always be there to support us. Based on what we discussed above, trust does become weak or broken at some point in a relationship when a partner fails to honor their word. But as much as we are in pain, we have developed a soft spot for our partner. We know they didn't do this intentionally, so we want to trust them, but it doesn't seem easy. To help you overcome this problem and rebuild the trust in your relationship, we've listed five different techniques below.

Take Baby Steps

Trust is not built overnight, neither in the beginning stages of your relationship nor the later stages. It takes time to have complete trust in your partner and be open with them. Remember when you met them for the first time? Did you immediately think you could trust them back then? No, you didn't. So, how can you expect to rebuild trust overnight? Going back through the entire process and rebuilding trust is more difficult due to the wounds left behind. Hence, you have to start taking small steps in the right direction. Try to be more open with them; tell them about your day and spend some time with them. With the help of your warm presence and attention, you will eventually be able to win their trust back if you were the one in the wrong. It takes time, so you will need to be patient while rebuilding that trust.

Be Honest With Them

Honesty is the best policy, especially if your partner's trust has been broken due to lies. You didn't mean to lie to them, but it just happened, and now you are stuck in this never-ending loop. When your partner discovers the lies, they are bound to be shattered. However, there is a way around this. You have to start being more honest with them. Share whatever details you need to; come clean to them and spill all your emotions. When a partner watches you in your vulnerable state, they will soften their heart and learn to trust you over time. When a partner becomes aware of your honesty and faithfulness, the road is paved for rebuilding the trust in your relationship.

Only Make Promises You Can Fulfill

Broken promises are also why partners develop trust issues, as we have highlighted previously. Sometimes we make promises we can't keep because we want to satisfy our partners. *Just this once let it go, and I promise I'll make it next time.* The next time never comes, and this results in issues. The best way to avoid this would be to only make promises you can fulfill. If you can't make it to the family dinner, don't make any promises. You know the date night has to be canceled tomorrow because you are working overtime, so don't promise your partner otherwise. Our partners will understand the situation, and they may be more than willing to let it go; lying, breaking promises, and abandoning them isn't the right way. To rebuild trust, you will have to learn to show up with your partner. Go to that family dinner, take them out on a date, spend time with them, show them that they are your priority, and eventually, they will slowly learn to trust you.

These three ways are simple techniques to gain trust. As always, communication is another way to build trust between partners. Openly talk to each other about the issues; why you couldn't fulfill the promise, why you lied about something, etc. This will give your partner a better understanding of the situation, and this way, you can heal the broken trust in the initial stages before things get worse. What we've discussed are the most basic things. Let us now talk about how developing a safe environment can help rebuild trust in relationships.

Developing a Safe Environment for Your Partner

Every relationship should have something known as the "safe space," where the couple can open up to each other without fear of judgment or criticism. When a partner feels that the other half will criticize their thoughts or actions, they will open up less, which can create trust problems in a relationship, as we saw. To repair the broken trust, you have to create a safe environment for your partner where they can learn to open up to you. In Chapter 1, we spoke about how trauma victims have difficulty trusting people. A broken trust is also a minor form of emotional trauma that makes people afraid their partner won't live up to their commitments or be honest with them. Developing a safe space seems like a viable option to dispel these fears, but how do you do it? Here are some of the ways you can create a safe space to rebuild trust in your relationship.

Leave Judgment at the Door

To create a safe space, you must leave all the negative emotions, including judgment, outside the door. Please don't bring it in and leave that baggage with your partner. Every partner has these small things they haven't told you because they are either embarrassed or unable to trust you. When you enter a safe environment, you ensure that your partner can potentially open up to you and tell you everything. This is especially comforting when you don't judge your partner because they can see that you understand them and feel the unconditional love emanating from you.

Don't Be Toxic

Safe space is also your partner's comfort zone, which at times they may use to vent their frustration. They are unleashing their annoyance buried deep within, and in these moments you may suddenly decide to disregard them. When a partner feels disrespected, they will never open up to you again. *He never takes it seriously. She always starts complaining about her life instead of paying attention.* Being toxic in these ways can affect your partner and they may choose not to openly talk to you next time. So when you enter a safe space, ensure that you will not talk back to them or mock them for trying to be honest with you.

Respect Their Boundaries

Every relationship should have a boundary where partners learn to respect each other. If a partner is always crossing their limits by insulting their other half, it will damage the relationship. Even when you enter the safe zone, you must always respect your partner's boundaries. Please don't be too clingy. Never force them to talk. When a partner realizes that their other half respects them and their boundaries, they will automatically communicate with you and tell you about their experiences.

All these things are small yet are the most impactful ways to build a safe space for your partner and repair trust. Additionally, we mentioned some other techniques like respecting your partner, listening to them carefully, and talking in a calm tone. All these factors show love and trust, and that this relationship means everything to you. In the next section, we will be touching upon how to check in with your partner to build a stronger bond.

Checking in With Your Partner to Build Trust

When I talk about 'checking in,' I mean that you have to make some time to approach your partner and have a light conversation. We are so busy with our lives every day that we become unaware of the challenges our partners may be facing. Your partner isn't always going to open up and share their problems. Some partners don't want to be a burden and avoid sharing anything negative with you. But it all gets exhausting for them, and then they go back to where you started—the fights, arguments, and the blame game. A check-in helps you overcome these obstacles by simply communicating with your partner. When we talk about check-in, you don't have to talk about feelings and how horrible your day has been going. You can get a bit creative here and ask a variety of questions to your partner to improve the relationship.

The amount of check-in you need depends on the health of your relationship. Some of us check in every day with basic things like: "Did you sleep well?" "How has your day been?" "What did you have for lunch?" This is one way to start a conversation with your partner and discover what they do during the day. If you like to check in every week or two, that works as well. "How was your week?" "Did you discover something new this week?" Something like this is like reflecting and expressing yourself in front of your partner. The questions listed above are some of the simple ones. We will be listing some creative questions in the workbook which you can ask your partner during the check-in process.

Why Is Check-In Important?

Checking in with your partner is one way to tell them "I am here for you." As I previously mentioned, many partners avoid talking about themselves because they feel guilty or don't want to burden you. When you check in with them, you allow them to open up to you. Some partners wish to share their painful feelings but fail to open up, as we discussed in Chapter 2 about communication breakdown. When you approach them this way, they can open up to you and tell you about what they feel. Just check in with your partner next time at the end of the day, asking, "How was your day?" They may reply something along the lines of "good," "bad," or "meh," but either way, you will learn how they are feeling and whether anything needs to be addressed.

Check-in highlights another important factor by showing how much you care and value your partner. We are familiar with the phrase "action speaks louder than words." In this case, when you check in with your partner, it shows how you care. Just simply asking questions like "Did you have your dinner yet?" shows you care about their wellbeing. Some partners might find it petty; however, most are happy to be checked in on. You can always create a check-in schedule and discuss it with your partner. Plus, check-in is one form of quality time you spend with your partner, which helps you communicate and thrive in a healthy relationship. Building trust and checking in are both essential factors that must be addressed in every relationship to strengthen the bond.

Throughout this book, we have learned about various issues and strategies, like the fundamental concept of how the brain thinks differently, the process of communication breakdown, the trust issues in a relationship, making mistakes that hurt your partner, ignoring your partners' needs, being in an emotional state, and more. We also went the extra mile and found various techniques to help you overcome these problems. Now that we are theoretically aware of these, it is time to show how they work in real life. In the next chapter, we will be discussing the outcome of all these techniques that we learned and how it has improved the relationship between our couple. Lastly, we will discuss how we can build a better future for our relationship through these techniques.

Key Takeaways

- Trust issues occur in any relationship and act as barriers between the couple. Rebuild trust by taking small steps, always being honest, and keeping all your promises.

- Creating a safe space to repair your partner's broken trust will help them understand that you accept their feelings and understand them.

- When you check in with your partner, they feel your care and affection toward them, allowing them to express themselves and have a conversation freely.

Application Workbook—6

Checking in on Your Partner

Checking in with your partner is another way you spend quality time with your partner, which should be utilized wisely. Take this time to ask them great questions, which will help you learn new things about them. Some of the questions that you can ask include:

- Are you feeling anxious about something lately?
- Are there any changes that you wish to make in our relationship?
- Is there anything you feel grateful about every day?
- Do you feel safe in this relationship?
- Have I done something to upset you lately?
- Are you facing any problems at your work or in your personal life?

These are some example questions, but you can expand your horizons. If you are going to discuss a sensitive topic, it is always better to give them a filler. Let them know in advance by saying, "Hey, can we talk about something that is bothering me?" After this, you can openly express yourself politely. No matter what your partner answers, be sure to resolve conflicts so that you can use this technique to build a healthy relationship with them.

Chapter 7:

Step 7–Reinventing Yourselves

Noah and Emma have had their ups and downs during their relationship. After falling in love and getting married, they fought every day. These fights severely damaged their relationship to nearly the point of no reconciliation. They both finally thought this was the end of their relationship after two years of togetherness. But hope came in the small form of this book. They discovered the various techniques listed in this book and realized there was space to heal their relationship. In this chapter, we will be discussing their journey and how our golden couple was able to work through their relationship problems.

Pulling It All Together

Emma and Noah were exhausted from all the problems that just kept coming one after the other. They couldn't cope in their relationship anymore. Emma would often think, *I wish I could escape somewhere.* Whereas Noah thought, *I'd be better off without all this drama.* They were standing against each other instead of being united against their problems. One day, Emma was reading something and she came across this quote from an anonymous person, "He can't read your mind. So take a moment to let him know how you feel." It struck her down like lightning that till now, she had been bottling her feelings and only expressing them when there was an ugly fight. Emma realized something, and if there was anything she could do to heal this relationship, it was to communicate.

Emma goes to the living room to find Noah sitting on the couch. She walks in and stands in front of him to get his attention. Once Noah notices her, he looks at her. She says, "Hey, do you think we could talk for a minute?" Noah nods in affirmation, letting her know it's okay to talk. "Noah, I am sorry for always unleashing my feelings on you as soon as you enter the house. I don't intend to start fighting with you after a long day. Some days, I feel so frustrated thinking about what is happening in this relationship. We barely talked or spent time together due to other commitments, which got to me. I just wanted to talk about it that day, but instead, it led to another major confrontation. I am sorry about arguing with you, and I would like to clear this up so that we can spend more meaningful time with each other."

Noah finally understood what went wrong that day and told Emma, "Hey Em, I am sorry, too. I just walked away from you and even said some hurtful words at times. It was never my intention to hurt you. I feel frustrated, too, you know. I am tired of overworking every day and barely having any time with you. I wish we could spend more time talking and hugging than screaming in each other's faces. I understand now what you must have gone through, and I am sorry. I would love to spend some quality time with you as well."

We finally start to see some form of reconciliation between Emma and Noah. Although this is only the beginning, there is hope that the couple will finally work out their issues and heal their relationship.

The Art of Rekindling the Fire: How Do We Build Our Future Together?

After the initial stages of reconciliation, Noah and Emma started adapting the techniques more and more into their relationship. For example, if Emma was ever upset about something, she would try and express it in a calm tone instead of directly confronting Noah and complaining about his behavior. At the same time, Noah would get easily frustrated sometimes, and he would give a pause signal to his partner, letting her know that he needed some time to cool down. They would keenly listen to each other talk and do their best to prioritize one another. Some days, Noah would come home early and take Emma on a date night, and other days both would stay in and enjoy their favorite movie together. Slowly, they were able to heal their broken relationship and go back to the passionate phase when they fell in love all over again.

Noah would sometimes come home and excitedly share things about his day and how he was excited about what was coming. Looking at the sparkle in his eyes, Emma would get happy, and she would also share all her happy moments. They were slowly able to stop clinging to small things that led to arguments. They would check in on one another and ensure that they were expressing themselves in front of their partner. There were more meaningful conversations where both would laugh and fewer arguments. If one of them made some mistake, they would apologize while the other person learned to forgive them. All these small actions that were missing in their relationship before helped them strengthen their bond.

With the help of these techniques, they both agreed and decided that if something went wrong, they would always communicate with each other. When one of them was frustrated, the other would remain calm and not fight with them. This way, they both decided to work through their issues, understand each other, and remain in a healthy relationship.

As we approach the end of this book, it may feel like we are coming to an end with this journey; however, it is just the beginning of a new stage in your healthy relationship. I hope this book helps you to overcome all your problems in your relationship and to heal your bond with your significant other.

Key Takeaways

- Communication and understanding is the easiest and simplest way to build a healthy relationship with your partner.

- Listening earnestly, forgiving quickly, validating emotions, and building an iron trust all hold significant value in your relationship.

Conclusion

Couples are having a hard time these days building successful and lasting relationships due to lack of understanding, fights, and different perspectives. In relationships, fights are inevitable and you need to learn how to work through these issues using the best course of action. We have already seen how many people are victims of past trauma or suffer from this constant anxiety, which makes it very difficult to express themselves in a relationship. Through this seven-step guide, our only goal was that we learn to put aside our differences, overwhelming feelings, and misunderstandings so that we can build and grow together.

Noah's and Emma's relationship was an example of what can go wrong and how we can get back up. At first, they misunderstood each other, but understanding brain mechanics helped them understand their differences. One was a thinker while the other was a feeler. Slowly, they began to see there was a huge gap in their communication and that they needed to close it. There would be fights and misunderstanding without clear communication. Emma took a step back and decided to listen to Noah for once. Noah could see the effort she was putting in, so he expressed himself freely. Both of them communicated with each other and realized that the cracks in their relationship were caused by their own negligence and lack of understanding for one another.

In the beginning, things slowed down as they argued a lot, but techniques like pressing the pause button, contemplating their feelings, and talking to each other often cleared their heads. Both of them learned to forgive each other and they developed an iron trust to strengthen their bond by using different strategies in this book. It took some time, baby steps as they say, but they finally took their first step to developing a healthy relationship.

Just like Noah and Emma, now is your chance to walk through this journey and build a healthy relationship with your partner. It doesn't matter where you are right now or what you are doing, take this opportunity to strengthen your bond with your partner. Express your feelings, treat them gently, communicate politely, love them deeply, and, most importantly, respect them. They are the same person who will be holding your hand and walking with you on this journey.

As we approach the end of this book, I would like to say this isn't the end but the beginning of a new phase in your relationship. With the help of this book, our goal was that you learn to rebuild your relationship with your partner and love them unconditionally. I hope all the techniques and the workbook exercises have helped you overcome obstacles and remain united in your relationship. If this book has helped you in any way or improved your relationship with your partner, please leave positive feedback, as it would mean the world to us.

References

Adahan, M. (2009, November 6). *Male brain, female brain.* Chabad.org. https://www.chabad.org/blogs/blog_cdo/aid/981317/jewish/Male-Brain-Female-Brain.htm

All Pro Dad. (2010, March 22). *10 ways to improve communication in marriage.* https://www.allprodad.com/10-ways-to-improve-communication-in-marriage/

All Pro Dad. (2016, October 19). *10 common communication breakdowns in marriage.* https://www.allprodad.com/10-common-communication-breakdowns-in-marriage/

Berman, H. (n.d.). *12 signs you and your partner are a total power couple.* FairyGodBoss. https://fairygodboss.com/career-topics/power-couple

Bonior, A. (2018, December 12). *7 ways to build trust in a relationship.* Psychology Today. https://www.psychologytoday.com/us/blog/friendship-20/201812/7-ways-build-trust-in-relationship

Brown, J. (2021, May 5). *Fix these 5 communication mistakes and your marriage will greatly improve.* Fatherly. https://www.fatherly.com/love-money/communication-mistakes-fixes-marriage/

Cafasso, J. (2019, May 17). *What part of the brain controls speech?* Healthline Media. https://www.healthline.com/health/what-part-of-the-brain-controls-speech#parts-of-the-brain

Campbell, S. M., & Grey, J. (2015). *Five-minute relationship repair: Quickly heal upsets, deepen intimacy, and use differences to strengthen love.* HJ Kramer.

Cassella, C. (2021, October 3). *9-Year study reveals the lasting effects childhood trauma has on adult relationships.* ScienceAlert. https://www.sciencealert.com/large-9-year-study-reveals-the-lingering-effects-of-childhood-trauma-on-adult-well-being

Centerstone. (n.d.). *11 tips for happier relationships.* https://centerstone.org/our-resources/health-wellness/tips-for-happier-relationships/#:~:text=Listening%20strengthens%20relationships%20and%20demonstrates

Craig, H. (2021, December 6). *10 ways to build trust in a relationship.* PositivePsychology.com. https://positivepsychology.com/build-trust/

Das, D. (2020, October 17). *How childhood trauma can affect your relationships.* The Times of India. https://timesofindia.indiatimes.com/life-style/relationships/love-sex/how-childhood-trauma-can-affect-your-relationships/articleshow/78675520.cms#:~:text=Researches%20have%20concluded%20that%20childhood

Denniswagenaar. (2021, December 5). *Thinker or feeler test: Are you a thinker or a feeler?* ProProfs Quiz. https://www.proprofs.com/quiz-school/story.php?title=thinking-vs-feeling-mbti-preference-3

Dr. Kolakowski, S. (2012, November 20). *The single best thing you can do for your relationship.* HuffPost. https://www.huffpost.com/entry/relationship-advice_b_2127394

Evans, M. (2020, December 7). *A quick guide: Checking in with your partner.* Shift Collab. https://www.shiftcollab.com/blog/a-quick-guide-checking-in-with-your-partner

Everyday Power. (n.d.). *150 relationship quotes celebrating real love.* https://everydaypower.com/best-relationship-quotes/

106

Gates Counseling. (2018, September 24). *Five ways to check in with your partner.* https://gatescounseling.com/five-ways-to-check-in-with-your-partner/

Gudisa, S. (2020, September 15). *Communication tips: How to harness the power of pause.* Enterprisersproject.com. https://enterprisersproject.com/article/2020/9/communication-tips-how-harness-power-pause

Gupta, S. (2021, December 27). *How to build trust in a relationship.* Verywell Mind. https://www.verywellmind.com/how-to-build-trust-in-a-relationship-5207611

Hall, K. (2012, April 26). *Understanding validation: A way to communicate acceptance.* Psychology Today. https://www.psychologytoday.com/us/blog/pieces-mind/201204/understanding-validation-way-communicate-acceptance

Healthline. (2021, November 30). *Frontal lobe anatomy & pictures.* https://www.healthline.com/human-body-maps/frontal-lobe

Kaiser, S. (2016, May 10). *7 keys to a happy relationship.* Live Happy. https://www.livehappy.com/relationships/7-keys-to-a-happy-relationship

Karrisa King Counselling. (2018, July 3). *Communicate better in your marriage: Male/Female brain differences.* http://www.karissakingcounseling.com/2018/07/03/communicate-better-in-your-marriage-male-female-brain-differences/

Kelloway, R. (2021, October 7). *Married to someone with childhood trauma? How it affects relationships.* Life Care Wellness. https://life-care-wellness.com/married-to-someone-with-childhood-trauma-how-it-affects-relationships/

Legato, M. J. (2017, March 23). *9 strategies to get your man to listen to you.* Prevention. https://www.prevention.com/life/g20455847/9-strategies-to-get-your-man-to-listen-to-you/

Marin, V. (2016, June 6). *The 10 most common things couples fight about, according To a sex therapist.* Bustle. https://www.bustle.com/articles/165111-the-10-most-common-things-couples-fight-about-according-to-a-sex-therapist

Martin, S. (2016, January 21). *The 11 biggest communication mistakes couples make.* Bustle. https://www.bustle.com/articles/135756-the-11-biggest-communication-mistakes-couples-make

Moheban-Wachtel, R. (2015, July 23). *10 ways to get your partner to listen (that don't involve yelling).* MBG Relationships. https://www.mindbodygreen.com/0-20809/10-ways-to-get-your-partner-to-listen-that-dont-involve-yelling.html

Olmedo, J. (2014, April 25). *How to validate your partner's feelings.* MyTherapyNYC - Counseling & Wellness. https://mytherapynyc.com/validate-partners-feelings/

Pace, R. (2020, November 20). *How to heal from relationship trauma.* Marriage.com. https://www.marriage.com/advice/mental-health/how-to-heal-from-relationship-trauma/

Pace, R. (2021, March 25). *4 common communication problems in marriage that you must know.* Marriage Advice - Expert Marriage Tips & Advice. https://www.marriage.com/advice/communication/4-common-communication-problems/

Pascale, R., & Primavera, L. (2019, April 25). *Male and female brains.* Psychology Today. https://www.psychologytoday.com/us/blog/so-happy-together/201904/male-and-female-brains#:~:text=The%20male%20brain%20is%20wired

Psych Central. (2021, July 26). *How to create emotional safety in a relationship: 7 tips.* https://psychcentral.com/blog/how-do-you-create-emotional-safety-in-your-relationships#how-to-create-it

Raab, D. (2017, August 9). *Deep listening in personal relationships.* Psychology Today. https://www.psychologytoday.com/intl/blog/the-empowerment-diary/201708/deep-listening-in-personal-relationships

Raypole, C. (2020, April 17). *Your partner is going to get on nerves — Here's how to work it out.* Healthline. https://www.healthline.com/health/coronavirus-pandemic-stress-anxiety-relationship#quick-tips

San Cristobal, P., Santelices, M. P., & Miranda Fuenzalida, D. A. (2017). *Manifestation of trauma: The effect of early traumatic experiences and adult attachment on parental reflective functioning.* Frontiers in Psychology, 8(449). https://doi.org/10.3389/fpsyg.2017.00449

Sangwin, B. (2016, December 29). *How forgiveness can transform your marriage.* The Gottman Institute. https://www.gottman.com/blog/forgiveness-can-transform-marriage/

Sorensen, M. S. (2017a). *I hear you: the surprisingly simple skill behind extraordinary relationships.* Autumn Creek Press.

Sorensen, M. S. (2017b, December 20). *Validation: The most powerful relationship skill you were never taught.* Michael S. Sorensen. https://michaelssorensen.com/validation-the-most-powerful-relationship-skill-you-were-never-taught/

Speakeasy Inc. (2016, February 12). *The power of the pause - Making silence work for you.* https://www.speakeasyinc.com/the-power-of-the-pause-making-silence-work-for-you/#:~:text=Allowing%20brief%20silences%20during%20communication

Stahl, K. (2019, May 20). *I use this question to check in with my spouse, and it's changed our relationship.* Popsugar Family. https://www.popsugar.com/family/How-Check-Your-Partner-46128676

Stritof, S. (2021, July 9). *Tips for rebuilding trust in your marriage.* Verywell Mind. https://www.verywellmind.com/rebuild-trust-in-your-marriage-2300999

The Church of Jesus Christ of Latter-day Saints. (2006). *Strengthening marriage instructor's guide.* https://www.churchofjesuschrist.org/bc/content/shared/content/english/pdf/language-materials/36889_eng.pdf

Thorp, T. (2019, July 12). *5 tips for improving your listening in a relationship.* Chopra. https://chopra.com/articles/5-tips-for-improving-your-listening-in-a-relationship

Treleaven, S. (2018, June 26). *The science behind happy relationships.* Time. https://time.com/5321262/science-behind-happy-healthy-relationships/

Urban, L. (2021, June 3). *How to be less emotional in a relationship.* WikiHow. https://www.wikihow.com/Be-Less-Emotional-in-a-Relationship

Vader, K. (2019, August 12). *Emotional intelligence in love and relationships.* Help Guide. https://www.helpguide.org/articles/mental-health/emotional-intelligence-love-relationships.htm

Well+Good. (2020, May 13). *I'm a couples therapist, and these are the 6 biggest communication issues I see in relationships.* https://www.wellandgood.com/communication-issues-in-relationships/

Zandan, N. (2013, June 19). *The power of pause.* Quantified. https://www.quantified.ai/blog/the-power-of-pause/

Zlotnick, S. (2021, August 3). *How to forgive your partner and move on after an argument.* Brides. https://www.brides.com/story/ways-to-forgive-your-spouse-after-a-major-fight

Printed in Great Britain
by Amazon